To Dr. Gordon D. Kaufman
my teacher and mentor

THE
COMMON
TASK

THE COMMON TASK

A THEOLOGY OF CHRISTIAN MISSION

M. THOMAS THANGARAJ

ABINGDON PRESS
NASHVILLE

THE COMMON TASK: A THEOLOGY OF CHRISTIAN MISSION

This book is printed on elemental-chlorine–free paper.

Library of Congress Cataloging–in–Publication Data

Thangaraj, M. Thomas (Melchizedec Thomas)
    The common task : a theology of christian mission / M. Thomas Thangaraj.
        p.   cm.
    Includes bibliographical references.
    ISBN 0-687-00144-7 (pbk. : alk. paper)
    1. Missions--Theory. I. Title.
BV2063.T34   1999
266'.001--dc21   98-31143
                                                          CIP

99 00 01 02 03 04 05 06 07 08 — 10 9 8 7 6 5 4 3 2 1

MANUFACTURED IN THE UNITED STATES OF AMERICA

Contents

Preface

While some eulogize the missionary expansion of the Christian church throughout the world and plead for a repetition of such an expansion, others consider the whole missionary enterprise a serious mistake and recommend that we delete the word "mission" from the Christian vocabulary itself. In reflecting as a Christian from India on the idea of mission, three things are clear in my mind. First, I am able to claim the Christian heritage for myself today because a group of missionaries from the Church of England along with some local evangelists preached the good news of Jesus Christ to my ancestors in South India, leading to their acceptance of the Christian faith. Acknowledging my history therefore leads me both to celebrate the Christian mission and to resolve to reflect on it with utmost seriousness and gratitude.

Second, as one who has experienced the Western missionary presence in India—both in the church and in the seminaries and as a student of the history of Christianity in India—I am aware of the ambiguities of the missionary enterprise as well. Growing up as a citizen of the independent nation of India and receiving Christian nurture from the Church of South India has instilled in me a critical eye that never fails to detect the problematic character of the church's missionary activity. Moreover, my active engagement with Hindus, Muslims, and others through programs of interreligious dialogue has exposed me to the bankruptcy of the traditional views of Christian mission. This has prodded me to rethink the idea of mission, so to speak, from the ground up.

Third, while acknowledging the problematic and ambiguous character of the missionary movement I am also mindful of the fact that the missionaries who came to my ancestral village had initiated a movement that promoted the liberation of those who were oppressed and exploited by both the religious and social forces around them. Thus the missionary task of the church has in most cases enabled personal and communal liberation. This historical fact should not be forgotten when one critically evaluates the modern missionary movement.

With these three concerns in mind, I began in 1988 to teach a course at the Candler School of Theology at Emory University on the theology of mission. The students who have enrolled in my course over the years have helped me to shape my missiological thinking in responsible and critical ways. My sincere thanks are due to all of them. The Dean and the Faculty of the Candler School of Theology have been supportive of my work with their collegiality and encouragement, and I express my gratitude to them. Furthermore, the Mission Resource Center of the General Board of Global Ministries of The United Methodist Church—housed on the Emory campus—offered me further opportunities to fine-tune my theology of mission. The staff and the missionary candidates at the Center interacted with me and sharpened my reflection on Christian mission. I am indebted to them all, especially to former director Milo Thornberry and present director Alan Kirton, who have helped me immensely in this process.

An early articulation of this theology of mission appeared in an essay entitled "Toward a Dialogical Theology of Mission," in *Theology at the End of Modernity*,[1] which is a collection of essays written in honor of Dr. Gordon D. Kaufman of Harvard University. Dr. Kaufman, my teacher and mentor, has significantly influenced my theological thinking over the years through his teaching, writing, and friendship. I find his theological method most suited for my own theological work as I engage the interreligious setting in which we find ourselves today. The reader should be able to detect easily the fact that this is a theology of mission that takes seriously into account Kaufman's theological method. Hoping to honor him and convey my heartfelt gratitude, I have dedicated this book to him.

Scott Jackson and Michael Brubaker helped me at various stages in the making of this book through the years 1996 to 1998 while each served as my research assistant. I am truly thankful to them both. Finally, I am grateful to my wife Cecilia and our children Raja and Naveena for their love and care that has sustained me through the years of research and teaching.

Introduction

The task of constructing a theology of mission during the days leading up to the twenty-first century is significantly different from what it would have been immediately after the dawn of the twentieth. The World Missionary Conference that met at Edinburgh, Scotland, in 1910 very appropriately represented the spirit and mood of those who reflected on the idea of the mission of the church at the beginning of this century. Edinburgh 1910, as it came to be known thereafter, was one of the most historic and dramatic events in the history of the Protestant missionary movement of the past three centuries. Nearly 1,200 delegates from 160 mission societies and Christian communities came from different parts of the world to attend this international conference. It was the first time this many official representatives of missionary societies (Protestant, of course) had met together, representing not only different Christian denominations but a wide number of the different nations of the world as well. They met for ten days and deliberated on several themes relating to the evangelization of the whole world. At the end of the conference, the delegates drafted two messages, one to "the members of the Church in Christian lands" and another to "the members of the Christian Church in non-Christian lands." The major thrust of the conference, as well as the two messages with which it concluded, was an invitation to Christians around the globe to join in the task of evangelizing the entire world. This invitation to unity, the most significant legacy of Edinburgh 1910, strengthened the ecumenical movement and ultimately led to the formation of the World Council of Churches in 1948. Edinburgh 1910 continued its missional emphasis in the work of the International Missionary Council, which was established in 1921 and merged with the World Council of Churches (WCC) in 1961 to form the Commission on World Mission and Evangelism within the WCC. From 1910 onward similar World Mission conferences were held in different parts of the world, the most recent being the 1996 conference in Salvador, Brazil. For our purposes here, I want to draw upon two aspects of the World Missionary Conference of 1910 to highlight the difference between the situation in 1910 and ours in the 1990s.

Circle of Discussion

First, let us consider the composition of the twelve hundred delegates who attended Edinburgh 1910. All but seventeen were European or North American.[1] Though most of this overwhelming majority had lived and worked at some time outside of Europe and North America or were doing so at the time, nonetheless only seventeen out of twelve hundred delegates were Christians from these "other lands." One should not fail to note that these seventeen men played an important part in the life of the conference, and quite a few of them addressed the assembly. One of them was the Rev. V. S. Azariah, who later became the first Indian bishop of the Anglican Church in India. Though some of these seventeen nonwhite delegates made significant contributions to the thinking of the conference, the major partners in the dialogue were the Europeans and Americans. Another important factor to be noted is that an overwhelming majority of the delegates were men. Among the twelve hundred delegates only a little fewer than two hundred were women. No woman gave the Evening Addresses that formed a valuable part of the conference proceedings. Most of the women delegates came as representatives from mission societies and mission programs that worked primarily among women. Nonetheless, the women who participated did play an important role in bringing to the agenda of the Conference the issue of the role and place of women in mission.[2]

After seventy-nine years, when the World Mission Conference of the Commission on World Mission and Evangelism of the World Council of Churches met in San Antonio, Texas, the scenario was profoundly different from Edinburgh 1910. Out of the 649 delegates representing 104 nations of the world, 70 percent came from Asia, Africa, Latin America, the Caribbean, the Middle East, and Eastern Europe.[3] Those present at this conference literally could see the colorful array of the different peoples of the world. A significant part of the leadership was in the hands of those who came from non-European and non-American countries. Quite an impressive difference from Edinburgh 1910! Moreover, 44 percent of the delegates to San Antonio 1989 were women. Women's active participation and able leadership were highly visible during this conference. Furthermore, 14 percent of the total delegates were under the age of thirty-five, and the Conference was preceded by a Youth Conference, called Encuentro, in which youth from around the world met to plan their impact on and contribution to the mission conference.

It is crystal clear that the circle of discussion has widened tremendously during the past eighty years. The conversation on the mission of the church is no longer limited to Europeans and North Americans but has become a truly global conversation. This is not to imply that the only contributions of non-Westerners have come in recent years or that they were passive and docile as regards the theory and practice of missions during the years before and after Edinburgh 1910. That simply would be untrue. For example, Bishop V. S. Azariah of India, who attended Edinburgh 1910, had already founded two missionary societies in India called the Indian Missionary Society of Tinnevelly and the National Missionary Society, both of which were committed to engage in mission within India using only local resources. In the same way women have always participated actively in the mission of the church and have reflected and articulated theologies of mission in profound ways.

What I am claiming here, therefore, is not that the peoples of the non-Western world had not reflected on the theology of mission until recently; rather, I am arguing that Christians from all parts of the world now have joined as equal and significant partners in the global conversation on the theology and practice of mission. The conversation is no longer limited to 475 Riverside Drive, New York![4] There was a time when a circle of discussion composed of North American missionaries and mission executives was falsely seen as a global discussion. Today the discussions taking place at 475 Riverside Drive at all times include women as well as persons from the non-Western world. For example, when the General Board of Global Ministries of The United Methodist Church discusses the theology of mission, people from different parts of the world are all present right there because the directors and staff of the Board themselves represent a wide variety of nations and cultures. This is true of most of the "mainline" Protestant mission agencies and societies. A similar situation prevails in the seminary and divinity school classrooms of the West. Students and teachers engaged in the task of reflecting on and articulating a theology of mission come from different parts of the world and include both men and women. As Rebecca Chopp rightly points out:

> One of the most significant changes in theological education in the last twenty years has been the dramatic rise in the number of women students. In some theological schools women make up more than 50 percent of the student body. In addition, the emergence of feminist theologies provides new discourses about women's lives, the nature of Christianity, and the substance of theology.[5]

There is yet another vital difference between Edinburgh 1910 and the situation today in terms of the composition of the circle of discussion. The conversation at Edinburgh was seen primarily as an intra-ecclesial one. It was a conversation among Christians about how they could best carry out the mission of the church in their time. The world was divided into two parts: Christian lands and non-Christian lands. The conversation was therefore primarily among Christians from "Christian lands," about the future of their missionary task in "non-Christian lands." Missionaries who were working among European and North American peoples were deliberately excluded and not invited to the conference. Though there were important deliberations on the role and place of world religions in the missionary task of the church, the conversation was purely an intra-Christian conversation.

During the past eight decades, the circle of dialogue has widened further to include so-called non-Christian believers, and so-called non-believers. People from religions other than Christianity have been invited to participate in and contribute to the conversation on understanding and articulating the mission of the church. When the World Council of Churches met in Vancouver, Canada, in 1983 for its General Assembly, representatives from such religions as Judaism, Hinduism, and Islam were invited to participate and to address the Assembly. The same was true of the next Assembly, which met in 1991 in Canberra, Australia. In these instances the circle of conversation was no longer limited to ecclesial communities; the wider circle included people from other religious traditions.

The discovery and development of the idea of "interreligious dialogue" as a form of missional presence in the world is a bold testimony to the willingness of Christians to discuss their missional call in the presence of and in interaction with people of other religions. When Stanley J. Samartha, a leading Christian theologian from India, was invited by the World Council of Churches to explore interreligious dialogue in 1968, the idea of dialogue with people of other religions was just beginning to attract the attention of those Christians involved in the missional task of the church. Since the inception of a separate sub-unit on "Dialogue with People of Other Faiths and Ideologies" within the Council, the idea of interreligious dialogue has been heavily debated in the churches all over the world. Whether people agree or disagree with the idea of "dialogue," this concept has come to assume a significant place in any discussion of the church's mission. Once "dialogue" becomes an important element in the articulation of mission, one cannot be satisfied simply with an intra-ecclesial conversation. The circle has to be widened; the conversation must be global.

The term "global," as I have thus far employed it, poses a problem. The way our argument has proceeded, I seem to assume that the pan-mainline-Protestant conversation is *the* "global" conversation. But this is only partially true. Both the Roman Catholic Church and the Orthodox Churches all over the world have in their own ways widened their circles of discussion in the past eight decades. Though the Roman Catholic Church has always functioned as a "global" church, one can say that only after Vatican II has the active participation of the Roman Catholic churches in the non-Western world become prominent. Roman Catholic theologians from non-Western areas have, in recent years, made more significant contributions to understanding the mission of the church than ever before in the history of the Roman Catholic Church.[6] Moreover, the participation of Roman Catholics in programs of the World Council of Churches also symbolizes the widening of the circle of discussion. The Orthodox Churches, who for a long time were suspicious of, and marginal to, the mission discussion in the West, have become vital partners in the conversation since 1961, when they became members of the World Council of Churches.

While we recognize the widening of the circle in both the intra-ecclesial and the interreligious setting, we also need to note an emerging polarization within the circle of conversation in the past twenty years or more. This polarization has occurred through the theological and political controversies between so-called ecumenicals and evangelicals since Edinburgh 1910. Missiologist David Bosch calls Edinburgh 1910 a "remarkable 'ecumenical evangelical' conference," and rightly so.[7] At Edinburgh there was no division between "ecumenicals" and "evangelicals," despite differences in theological perspectives and missional understandings. But during the past eighty years, the divide between evangelicals and ecumenicals has grown sharper and much more clearly defined.

Alienation and confrontation first entered ecumenical-evangelical relationships as the International Missionary Council became incorporated within the WCC and also as evangelicals became dissatisfied with the missional theology articulated by the Council's Commission on World Mission and Evangelism. Evangelicals detected a heavy and unhealthy influence of both liberation theologies and programs of interreligious dialogue on the theology of mission.[8] This confrontation led to the Lausanne Congress on World Evangelization in 1974, which was organized by evangelicals from all around the world. For the first time the evangelical voice on the theology of mission was heard with clarity and unity in a global setting. The *Lausanne Covenant*, the document prepared by the Congress, still serves as the definitive document that defines mission and evangelism for evangelicals across the world. The Congress met again at Pattaya, Thailand, in 1980 and at Manila, the Philippines, in 1989. Participants at both these meetings reiterated and strengthened the *Lausanne Covenant*.

Given this polarized situation, it is all the more necessary that evangelicals and ecumenicals enter one circle of discussion and engage in conversation on the theology and practice of Christian mission. Today's setting demands a widening of the circle of discussion to include people from different ecclesial families, ethnic and national groups, religious traditions, and theological perspectives.

Crisis of Confidence

The ethos that dominated the World Mission Conference at Edinburgh 1910 was one of confidence and optimism. The leadership of the conference came largely from those actively involved in the work of the Student Volunteer Fellowship. The Fellowship's motto was "the evangelization of the world in our own generation," a phrase that might be said to characterize the mood of Edinburgh 1910 as a whole. David Bosch ably traces this optimism and confidence back to the Enlightenment. As he writes, "More than in any preceding period, Christians of this era believed that the future of the world and of God's cause depended on *them.*"[9] Bosch then quotes a long piece from the writings of John R. Mott, one of the leaders of Edinburgh 1910, commenting that

> [These writings convey] the spirit of optimism and confidence that characterized Western, especially North American, missionary circles at the beginning of our century. It was this spirit that prevailed also at the Edinburgh conference. Edinburgh represented the all-time high water mark in Western missionary enthusiasm, the zenith of the optimistic and pragmatist approach to missions.[10]

This enthusiasm was reflected equally in the messages that went forth from the Conference at Edinburgh. For example, the message of the conference addressed "to the members of the Church in Christian lands" goes like this:

> Our survey has impressed upon us the momentous character of the present hour. We have heard from many quarters of the awakening of great nations, of the opening of long-closed doors, and of movements which are placing all at once before the Church a new world to be won for Christ. The next ten years will in all probability constitute a turning-point in human history, . . . if they are rightly used, they may be among the most glorious in Christian history.[11]

Let me give one more illustration of this confidence from the closing address by John R. Mott. Mott's remarks are both eloquent and extremely hopeful of the days to come.

> Our best days are ahead of us and not in these ten days that we have spent together, still less in the days that lie behind them. Why? Because we go forth tonight with larger knowledge, and this in itself is a talent which makes possible better things. We go out with a larger acquaintanceship, with deeper realization of this fellowship which we have just

seen, and that is a rich talent which makes possible wonderful achievements. Our best days are ahead of us because of a larger body of experience now happily placed at the disposal of Christendom. . . . Therefore, with rich talents like these which we bear forth, surely our best days are ahead of every one of us, even the most distinguished person in our great company.[12]

Today, in contrast, we live in a markedly different situation. The optimism about human progress and the confidence about the "evangelization" of the *whole* world have been toned down significantly by the events that have taken place since 1910. These events, along with the demographic, cultural, social, and political changes that have accompanied them, have helped us to be slow and cautious in foretelling the future of the church's mission in the world. Let me discuss briefly several of these events and changes.

World Wars I and II have had significant impact on the confidence of Christian theologians. These two tragic wars demonstrated very clearly the depth of human sin and the power of human hubris. These wars demonstrated that humans, while making progress in science, technology, and other fields, are nonetheless very capable of engaging in extreme forms of violence and cruelty. Not simply as individuals but also as groups and nations, we demonstrated our utter sinfulness in these two wars. The Western missionaries who were working in different parts of the non-Western world found themselves on opposite sides of the war and had to deal with the problem of enmity and hostility among themselves. Human progress, though seen as a great ally to the missionary movement at the beginning of the century, was no longer a trusted ally in the task of evangelizing the whole world. Rather, human progress itself needed to hear the prophetic word of the church's mission.

The Neo-Orthodox movement in Christian theology, as spearheaded by Karl Barth, Emil Brunner, and others, clearly articulated this lack of confidence in human nature during the period after World War I. Barth's attack on liberal Protestantism centered largely on its romantic understanding of the human; thus, his repeated emphasis on God as "Wholly Other" laid bare the tragic side of the human story. As Barth put it in the beginning of his commentary on Paul's Epistle to the Romans:

The Gospel proclaims a God utterly distinct from men. Salvation comes to them from Him, because they are, as men, incapable of knowing Him, and because they have no right to claim anything from Him.[13]

Thus, confidence in the efforts of humans to evangelize the whole world was chastened by a realistic understanding of the human predicament.

The second major development since Edinburgh 1910 has been the slow and steady "dismantling of the colonial framework."[14] The European colonialism of the past two centuries was viewed as an ally in the missionary task of the church until World War II. The history of the interaction of colonial expansion and the missionary enterprise has been a complex one. In the beginning the early European colonizers did not associate themselves with the church's missionary task. Although the Spaniards and Portuguese were exceptions to this rule,[15] the British objected to sending missionaries to the areas where they were heavily involved in commerce and trade. They saw the missionary enterprise as "a threat to their commercial interests."[16]

However, this separation of "mission" and "colonial expansion" did not last long. Growing public opinion in Europe and North America demanded the sending of missionaries to colonized areas. In this process, missionaries and colonizers saw themselves as assisting each other. Missionaries saw the West's colonial expansion as God's own providential way of opening the doors for preaching the gospel in the uttermost parts of the earth. Similarly colonizers saw missionary work as a way of subduing people in the colonies. One illustration suffices to demonstrate this alliance between missionaries and colonizers.

Missionary stations are the most efficient agents which can be employed to promote the internal strength of our colonies, and the cheapest and best military posts that a wise government can employ to defend its frontier against the predatory incursions of savage tribes.[17]

Yet not all missionaries saw colonizers as their allies. It is too simplistic to see the missionary movement and colonial expansion as neatly parallel developments. The independence movements in various colonies were greatly assisted by the work of the missionaries in those areas. Thus, when we assert that colonialism was seen as an ally for the missionary task of the church, we must do so with the three qualifications mentioned above.

After World War II the nations in Asia and Africa that were under European political control began one after another to gain independence. The independence movements saw both colonial expansion and the missionary enterprise as expressions of Western imperialism and triumphalism. The "Heyday of Colonialism," (i.e. the period from 1858 to 1914) as Stephen Neill calls it, came to an end with the two World Wars.[18] This "dismantling of colonialism" brought a lack of confidence in the "evangelization of the world in our own generation" that was echoed in Edinburgh 1910.

The third major development in the post-1910 period has been the resurgence and renaissance of religions other than Christianity. But the resurgence of which I speak did not simply occur after 1910; it had started at the time when Christian missions had begun their work in the non-Western world. For example, during the nineteenth century Hinduism went through a great revival and renaissance, especially through the work of such Hindu reformers as Raja Ram Mohan Roy, Swami Vivekananda, and others. Yet only after 1910 did missionaries take serious note of this resurgence. In describing the mood of Edinburgh 1910, Stephen Neill writes:

> The delegates [to Edinburgh 1910] differed somewhat in their attitude towards the non-Christian religions; but all were agreed that, as the lordship of Christ came to be recognized, these other religions would disappear in their present form—the time would come when Siva and Vishnu [Hindu gods] would have no more worshippers than Zeus and Apollo have today. Expression of these views might differ a little in detail; it cannot be questioned that in 1910 there was practical unanimity with regard to the substance of them.[19]

Such a confidence in the demise of non-Christian religions no longer persists in most missionary circles today. Religions other than Christianity have revitalized themselves precisely through their encounter with Christianity. For example, Hinduism has reconstructed itself as a missionary religion and started sending missionaries to the West. The popularity of Hindu gurus in Europe and North America and the growth of ISKCON in the West symbolizes such a resurgence of Hinduism.

If this renaissance of religions other than Christianity had been contained geographically within the nations of Asia, Africa, and Latin

20

America, its effect on missionary confidence would not have become as significant as it is today. But this resurgence is coupled with the migration of people belonging to religions other than Christianity into Western societies and nations. Let me illustrate this point with two cities. First, Atlanta, site of the 1996 Olympic Games, is experiencing the revival of several religions within its own landscape. In preparation for the hosting of the Games, Gary Laderman, a historian of religions at Emory University, edited a book entitled *Religions of Atlanta: Religious Diversity in the Centennial Olympic City.*[20] In this book Laderman, with the help of several other scholars, presents us with a clear picture of the religious landscape of Atlanta. Introducing the theme of religious diversity, Laderman has this to say:

> Soon after Atlanta first came into existence in the 1830s as a railroad terminus, one building served as the meeting space for different Protestant congregations in the area. Now, over a century and a half later, travel north, south, east, and west through metropolitan Atlanta and you will find multiple forms of religious life on almost every street. Homes, churches, synagogues, mosques, community centers, strip malls, office parks, sports arenas, and other venues are used as locations for religious instruction and an assortment of religious practices.[21]

On the same page, Laderman refers to the new situation as "Atlanta's religious marketplace." In addition to a plethora of Christian denominations, Atlanta now has nearly 40,000 Muslims, 20,000 Hindus, 500 Bahais, and more than 10,000 Buddhists living within the metropolitan area. Religious centers and places of worship belonging to these religious groups flourish. It is the Christian churches, mostly mainline Protestant, that suffer from a decline in membership and not these other religious groups. Such dramatic change in the religious landscape does affect the missionary confidence of the church. Second, let me offer one more illustration from another part of the world. The city of Birmingham in England, one of the largest Muslim cities outside the Middle East, has more than fifty mosques. The central mosque in the city is claimed to be the largest in Europe outside Istanbul.[22] Muslims form nearly 20 percent of the total population of Birmingham. Thus the new proximity of people of other religions and the novel religious landscape are bringing a new awareness of religious plurality.

This leads us to discuss the fourth development since 1910. There is widespread agreement among people of various religious traditions that we live in a time of novel and intense consciousness of religious plurality. It is a novel consciousness not because the world has suddenly—overnight, as it were—become more pluralistic in the variety of religious traditions. Religious plurality has always been a fact. Yet, this plurality is known, felt, and experienced today by more people than ever before. Several reasons account for this novel consciousness, but let me simply highlight two of them. First, the particularity and distinctiveness of each religious tradition has become more appreciated and understood. This has happened primarily because recently people from different religious traditions have begun to live in proximity to each other in the Western world (as the examples of Atlanta, Georgia, in the United States, and Birmingham, England, illustrate). Moreover, we have a new statistical awareness regarding religious plurality. For example, we are now very much aware that only 33 percent of the total population of the world is Christian in some form or another. Another way to look at the statistics is to imagine a global village and project its composition. The World Development Forum offers us this picture: "If you lived in a representative global village of 1,000, there would be . . .

- 300 Christians (183 Catholics, 84 Protestants and 33 Orthodox)
- 175 Moslems
- 128 Hindus
- 55 Buddhists
- 47 Animists
- 210 without any religion or confessed atheists
- 85 from other smaller religious groups." [23]

This novel consciousness is not limited to our demographic and statistical awareness of the multiplicity of religious traditions. If we were left to such demographic awareness alone, religious plurality would not pose any problem of significant intensity to the question of the mission of the church. But we are also keenly aware of the interconnectedness of human life in all its dimensions, including the political, social, economic, cultural, and environmental spheres. Advanced communications technology and transportation systems have brought the people of the world in closer proximity to each other. During my visit to Bangalore, India, in the summer of 1995, the fact of our interconnectedness came home to me very powerfully when I read the morning newspaper.

The Times of India clearly depicted a world which is interconnected and interdependent. The page on international news that day mentioned:

- $350 million of World Bank aid to India,
- Michael Jackson, the rock star,
- a Christian Dior fashion show,
- Israel-Palestine peace-negotiations,
- the debate over giving the most powerful handguns to police,

and so on. All these indicate how our stories and histories are inter-locked with each other. The listing of cable TV programs contained among others *Teenage Mutant Ninja Turtles, Urban Cowboy, The Oprah Winfrey Show,* and *Dynasty.* The TV channels in Bangalore include MTV and The Discovery Channel. The fact of global interconnectedness should never be forgotten when we think about relating to people of other faiths. All of our problems are global problems and demand global solutions. Such global solutions have to be worked out by the people of the whole world in consultation and cooperation with each other. The local and the global spheres have come to interact with one another in ways we could not previously imagine. This global interconnectedness is as much a matter of politics and economics as it is of communications technology. Thus, global problems have to be addressed by the global community, not simply one branch of it—even the Christian community. This means that Christians will be increasingly drawn into interaction and conversation with other religious communities in our mission to serve humanity. We are compelled to take the worldviews of other religionists more seriously than before, and this again has its impact on the way we look at the people of other religious traditions.

Our consciousness is not simply novel, it is also intense. There was a time when one would have looked at the question of multireligious reality simply as a matter of what one might call *anthropological curiosity.* The people of other religions appear to us as those who live in faraway lands with "exotic" customs and practices. They kindle our fascination for the strange and the unknown. In such a situation, an engagement with religious pluralism, even when it is passionate, is largely a matter of "detached" intellectual and "scientific" curiosity. Some even today may think of religious pluralism merely in the context of such anthropological curiosity.

But, interestingly, most people today do not limit themselves to an anthropological curiosity. Rather, they demonstrate what might be called an *existential anxiety* when it comes to the question of religious pluralism. This is an anxiety that arises out of the need to define one's identity in light of other religious traditions. What if I am wrong and they are right? If one is right, the other has to be wrong; so which one is right? My faith or theirs? Thus does the problem of self-identification give rise to existential anxiety.

There exists a further existential anxiety that is linked to questions of the Christian orientation to life, a situation of "intellectual anxiety" with regard to Christian beliefs and practices. This intellectual anxiety comes to the surface through the direct contact we have with the beliefs, practices, and lifestyles of other religious traditions. It is heightened by the decline of the centrality of the Christian faith in the life of the societies in the West. One is led more and more to see the Western societies as "mission fields." James Scherer calls this "the most serious of all [crises]: the *crisis of faith*, spirit, and the theological conviction in the Western world."[24] Lesslie Newbigin names this as "a profound crisis of faith within the Western Churches [that] has led to a loss of conviction that there is anything in the Christian faith which is so vital without it men will perish."[25]

Since the time of Edinburgh 1910, a novel and intense consciousness about religious pluralism has come into existence. This consciousness is expressed not merely through an anthropological curiosity that is fascinated by religious traditions other than one's own, but profoundly through an existential anxiety that confronts one with questions regarding one's own religious identity, challenges the traditional beliefs and practices in one's own religious tradition, and invites one to explore new forms of coexistence and cooperation with people of other religions. Such a shift in our consciousness of religious pluralism does affect our missionary confidence.

The fifth, and perhaps the most serious, development is the rise of postmodern thought. The term "postmodern" gained popularity first through the writings of French authors such as Jean-Francois Lyotard, Jacques Derrida, and Michel Foucault.[26] Postmodernism is an elusive concept; the very nature of postmodern thought is such that one cannot bring an all-encompassing concept to describe it. But for our purposes here let me simply provide some thoughts that point to the meaning of this far-reaching intellectual and cultural movement. Relying on

24

Lyotard's definition, one may say that postmodern thought is one that questions and deconstructs overarching narratives that govern our thinking about the multiplicity of events, ideas, and movements in history. Lyotard calls it an "incredulity towards metanarratives."[27] For example, people in the Western Christian culture have always understood their life and their place in the universe through the grand narrative supplied by the Jewish and Christian traditions. Fundamentally, it is a narrative about God and God's dealings with the whole universe. Postmodernism questions that "grand narrative" and discovers in its place multiple, smaller, and local narratives that are relative and subjective to the person or community who owns them as their narratives. This loss of a grand narrative leads to a viewing of the social reality in atomistic terms.

In his most recent book, Peter Hodgson sets before us seven different crises that are brought forth by postmodern thought. First of all, there is a "cognitive crisis" in which human reason is itself suspect. He writes:

> The first Enlightenment gave rise to a relativizing consciousness, but consciousness itself was not relativized. Now there appears no longer to be a universal logos, either religious or secular, and it is clear that thought and perception are more radically conditioned by perspective, circumstances, and interests than rationalism supposed.[28]

Second is an historical crisis in which the grand narratives such as Salvation History, the theory of scientific and technological progress, and the ideal of Communist eschaton have all collapsed in front of our eyes in this century. Third is the political crisis in which the West has lost its hegemony. Fourth, the failure of Marxist ideology and socialism has led to an economic crisis in which consumption-driven capitalism has come to control the economic activities around the globe. Fifth, "a crisis of the human spirit" has taken place through the destruction of the environment. Sixth, there is "a gender crisis — the beginning of the ending of patriarchy as a way of organizing male-female relations and distributing social power." Finally, there is today a religious crisis. Hodgson sees in this religious crisis three major and somewhat contradictory factors at work: the decline of Christianity in the West, the rise of violence in the name of religion, and an increasing number of instances of interreligious dialogue and cooperation.[29] All of these crises are the result of the loss of a grand narrative to describe, understand, and guide the human situation. The postmodern way of thinking brings forth a de-centering of thought and action, and such a de-centering makes the task of mission highly questionable and extremely difficult to articulate about and engage in.

What I have described so far is a list of events, ideas, and movements that have toned down the optimistic confidence of those who met at Edinburgh in 1910 in the "evangelization of the whole world" in one's generation. However persuasive my argument might have been in showing the crisis of confidence in the missionary task of the church, one should not fail to notice that a sizable number of Christians even today do not experience this kind of crisis. They often imagine themselves to be living in a world that is clearly defined to them in and through biblical narratives, and therefore they continue to be equally enthusiastic about the task of mission as they would have been in pre-1910 days. Even those who recognize the onslaught of postmodernism tend to see their task as turning back the clock to earlier times. As Hodgson writes, it is

> essentially an effort to stop the progress, turn the clock back — indeed to turn it back to pre-Enlightenment times, to traditional bases of authority and conventional forms of religious belief. The resurgence of conservative and evangelical Christianity in recent years is symptomatic both of the magnitude of the experienced threat and of the deep desire to recover stable ethical and religious foundations in a topsy-turvy age.[30]

For example, an evangelical scholar from India, in his recent book on mission, pleads for going back to biblical foundations and thus "regain our mission morale."[31]

There are others who, by taking the challenge of postmodernism seriously, do not see any way of going forward with the idea of mission. "Mission" belongs to a "grand narrative" that they, together with other postmodernists, have condemned as oppressive and unproductive. It belongs to a period when Christians, especially Western Christians, had identified their local and parochial story with the grand narrative and thus dealt with people of other races, nations, and cultures in highly imperialistic terms. I have met quite often, both in my classrooms and in the larger ecclesial communities, postmodern Christians who are so burdened by the negativities of the missionary era that they have no place for the word "mission" either in their spiritual vocabulary or in their academic exercise. The only option they can detect on the horizon is to sink into despair and fail to discover any new way of reinterpreting the missionary mandate of the church today.

What I am opting for is a third way of addressing the situation today. It is neither a desire to go back in history to the "good old" days of missionary expansion of the church nor an urge to wallow in the cynicism and nihilism that paralyzes us in our guilt. We need to ask ourselves afresh this question: What does the current situation—the widening of the circle of discussion, and the crisis of confidence in the mission of the church—mean for the construction of a theology of mission today? It clearly means that we cannot do "business as usual." Several shifts and changes will have to take place in our way of engaging in this construction. These shifts are not going to be simply marginal to the task of theological construction. These will affect the very method by which we go about constructing a theology of mission. While there may be several shifts and changes that must occur, I want to highlight three such changes that take seriously the postmodern critique of the Christian missiological enterprise.

First, it should be acknowledged straightforwardly that the word "mission" is no longer the private property of Christian discourse. It is a word in the English language and thus a word in normal human discourse. It is a public word. In earlier times, for example in India, the word "mission" was closely and often solely related to the work of the Christian churches in India. But today in the city of Madurai, South India, one comes across the Meenakshi Mission Hospital and the Hindu Mission Hospital.[32] Furthermore, the word "mission" is not in any way a peculiarly religious word either; national governments talk about their political mission, and even the popular fictional character James Bond 007 refers to his activity as a mission to be accomplished! Corporations and organizations are mandated these days to fashion their own "mission statement," which outlines and describes the task that is peculiar to their institution. So the public character of the word "mission" makes it possible for us to engage in a circle of discussion that is much wider than the ecclesial communities. The publicity of the word "mission" puts us in a context that is much broader and more complex

27

than Edinburgh 1910. It reflects the "global" community in which we find ourselves today. Such a recognition of the public character of "mission" has serious methodological implications for constructing a theology of mission. It compels us to do our theology in public and in the open marketplace of ideas and concepts. Where and how we will begin our construction, how we will proceed further in our reflection on mission, and other such questions become important in the process of constructing a theology of mission. I will discuss this detail in chapter 1. It is sufficient at this point to affirm that the public character of the term "mission" should be forthrightly acknowledged by missiologists.

Second, if we accept the postmodern critique of metanarratives as valid, we need to begin our theological construction with local stories. The local stories are of two kinds, namely, one's own autobiography and the story of one's own local community, however one may define "local" at that point. More and more scholars today are beginning to recognize the importance and value of autobiographical reflection as a theological method. For example, Mark K. Taylor's *Remembering Esperanza: A Cultural-Political Theology for North American Praxis* is an excellent christological exercise done in the setting of his autobiography.[33] Asian theologians like C. S. Song and Kosuke Koyama have articulated their theologies in and through the stories of Asian peoples.[34] The feminist and womanist theologians also have highlighted the need to theologize autobiographically.[35]

The very use of the word "mission" in our theological exercise then has to be defended autobiographically. I come from a small village in South India called Nazareth. Around the beginning of the nineteenth century, the people of my village welcomed Anglican missionaries into their midst, listened to the proclamation of the Gospel of Jesus Christ by those missionaries, and accepted the Christian faith in large numbers.[36] Such a mass conversion led to the renaming of their village as Nazareth. Though one may rightly criticize the modern missionary movement for its imperialism and for its subjugation and disfigurement of particular cultures in several parts of the world, the word "mission" for my people in Nazareth, South India, meant liberation, the flourishing of their human potential, and a regaining of their dignity and pride. These were people who belonged to the lower rungs of the Indian caste ladder, and for them "mission" meant freedom from oppression and ignorance.

This is not only the case with the people of Nazareth. It is true, to a large extent, of the wider society in India. The word "mission" has stood for service, compassion, and liberation. That is why Hindus in the city of Madurai do not find it problematic in any way to name their hospitals Hindu Mission Hospital and Meenakshi Mission Hospital. Given such perception of "mission" in my setting, I find that my story and my people's story in India gives me the freedom to pick up the word "mission" with confidence, work with it, and construct a theology of mission. I am no longer restricted or controlled by the post-Christian sense of guilt about the missionary enterprise that is so prevalent in the churches in the West.

The method of autobiography has another advantage as well. It enables theologians to be forthright in their acknowledgment of their own social location and particular standing. It allows them to take responsibility publicly for their work. Theology is *our* work, and it is *we* who do our theologies with our own stories and histories. This is manifested through the autobiographical methodology of theological reflection.

Third, if we bring our "local" stories into the task of theologizing, we need to guard against the possibility that our theologies might simply become matters of our inner subjectivity and autobiographical fancy. This means that our "local" stories need to be in conversation with each other in the task of constructing a theology of mission for today. The kind of widening of the circle of discussion that I had highlighted at the beginning of this introduction calls for conversation and dialogue. Only in an ever-widening conversation between Christians and others can one's theology of mission be worked out. This is demanded both by the width of the circle of conversation and by the seriousness of the crisis of confidence.

Here again, one can see how theologians of today are recognizing the importance of dialogue and conversation as a method in theology. Hodgson, in describing the three quests that are engendered by the postmodernist critique (emancipatory, ecological, and dialogical), has this to say about dialogue. He writes that dialogue

> prevents this circularity [that exists between beliefs and norms] from becoming a static, self-enclosed system by insisting that it is possible to bring alternative traditions into productive encounter with each other, thus keeping them dynamic, growing, open to transformation. Dialogue involves a spiraling toward new and always open possibilities, as opposed to the circularity of relativism and deconstruction and the linearity of essentialist views.[37]

Gordon Kaufman, another leading theologian in the North American scene, sees theology as a "free-flowing, open, and unfettered conversation." He writes:

> Free-flowing conversation presupposes a consciousness of being but one participant in a larger developing yet open-ended pattern of many voices, each having its own integrity, none being reducible to any of the others; and it presupposes a willingness to be but one voice in this developing texture of words and ideas, with no desire to control the entire movement. . . . In this model truth is never final or complete or unchanging; it develops and is transformed in unpredictable ways as the conversation proceeds.[38]

The conversational method in theology takes seriously the ever-widening circle of discussion and also acknowledges and respects the integrity of "local" stories.

Thus, this book's attempt at constructing a theology of mission operates with these three guiding principles, namely, the public character of the word "mission," the primacy of autobiographical reflection in the theological task, and the importance of conversation for and at every step of the constructive process.

Let me conclude by outlining the movement of this book. Chapter 1 aims to propose a new starting point, namely, an explication of the idea of the mission of humanity for constructing a theology of mission. This is followed by an exposition of the mission of humanity in chapter 2. The next chapter brings in the particularly Christian theological components to the idea of the mission of humanity and puts forward a basic framework for a theology of mission. In the following chapter I further explain the mission of the church by discussing the implications of this theology for areas such as evangelism, social action, and so on. Chapter 5 uses the idea of mission proposed in chapters 3 and 4 as a vantage point to reread the missionary history of the church in critical terms. A similar exercise is done in chapter 6 with regard to biblical materials that have been widely used in articulating the mission of the church. The final chapter provides some guidelines and suggestions as to how one may go about helping congregations to think about, plan for, and engage in meaningful mission today.

1

A New
Starting Point

We began our inquiry into the task of constructing a theology of mission by outlining the dramatic and highly significant changes that have occurred in recent times in the context of such theological construction. I noted that the circle of discussion has widened to include both Christians from all six continents and people who profess religions other than Christianity. We have seen further that the kind of confidence that traditionally undergirded the thinking on and the acting out of the church's mission is no longer available to us today. The postmodern critique of "grand narratives" has driven us to recover our "local" stories, and it has decreased our missionary confidence. I concluded this discussion by mentioning three specific moves necessary for constructing a theology of mission: the primacy of autobiographical reflection; the need for conversation across traditional boundaries; and the recognition of the "public" character of the word "mission."

Now the question before us is this: Given this widened circle of discussion, and the understanding of conversation as theological method, how shall we begin? Before I proceed to answer this question, I need to explicate the role of "conversation" in this project. I am using the idea of conversation as both a methodological and an epistemological category. As a methodological category it enables us to include "the other" in articulating a theology of mission. As Gadamer has suggested, the method of question and answer (which is primary for a conversation) can be used only when there are others present to engage in that conversation. He writes, "The first condition of the art of conversation is to ensure that the other person is with us."[1] Once the other is with us, we need to find a way in which our understanding of mission is open to questioning. Such openness demands that we move beyond the "historical horizon" that our view of mission grants to us. Gadamer, of course, makes these observations on conversation mainly in relation to the task of interpreting "texts." But we can see that those insights apply to our construction of a theology of mission as well. He explains that the text (seen as an answer) has to be submitted to a new set of questions that come out of a conversation. For such a conversation to happen, "we must attempt to reconstruct the question to which the transmitted text is the answer. But we shall not be able to do this without going beyond the historical horizon it presents us with.[2] Therefore, by choosing conversation as our method, we attempt to go beyond the "historical horizon" that our talk concerning mission has presented us with so far. This would involve discovering a different starting point for our missiological reflection than what we have done so far in our history.

I am using "conversation" as an epistemological category as well. Conversation is not only a method to include other voices; it is also a source of transformative knowledge. To quote Gadamer again: "To reach an understanding with one's partner in a dialogue is not merely a matter of total self-expression and successful assertion of one's own point of view, but a transformation into a communion, in which we do not remain what we were."[3] Elsewhere, Gadamer writes that "conversation has a spirit of its own" and thus "reveals something which henceforth exists."[4] Something novel appears in the midst of conversation and as the result of conversation. This view of conversation gives it a seriousness that we often do not give it in our common usage. For example, one might ordinarily assume conversation to be without any goals or limits, and that thus it has the potential of winding up empty. But what I mean here by conversation is a serious "engagement" with one another leading to fresh and novel knowledge. Because of this openness to the "other," we cannot predict at the beginning of the conversation what understandings of mission would result from this process.

If this is what we mean by conversation, how shall we begin the conversation on mission so that it will include people of other religious and ideological persuasions, continue and sustain an ongoing dialogue, and result in novel understandings of mission? Traditionally, our theologies have begun their articulation of mission with the Bible as the starting point. This was true not only of books on the *history* of mission; the same was the case for books that attempted to offer a fresh articulation of a contemporary *theology* of mission as well. Two presuppositions govern the rationale behind such a move. First, theology was seen primarily as hermeneutics of Christian scriptures. Second, biblical materials—those defined by the canon—were viewed as the primary, if not the only, source for articulating a theology of mission.

In this project, I am not taking the task of theology to be mere hermeneutics of sacred texts such as the Bible. Theology is much more than a "one-dimensional hermeneutical enterprise, limited entirely to the explication of texts; it has also always been critical and constructive in character, concerned with working out more adequate ways to conceptualize God."[5] Therefore I do not find it helpful to begin the discussion of mission with the Bible as the starting point. I am also operating, for several reasons, with the assumption that the Bible is not the *only* source for theological articulation. First, the frequent insistence in the history of Christian theology that Scripture be combined with tradition as the sources of theological construction and reflection bears witness to the problem we are referring to here. Second, most contemporary theologians include sources other than the Bible in their theological articulation. For example, Tillich writes:

> In dealing with the question of the sources of systematic theology, we must reject the assertion of neo-orthodox biblicism that the Bible is the *only* source. The biblical message cannot be understood and could not have been received had there been no preparation for it in human religion and culture. . . . Systematic theology, therefore, has additional sources beyond the Bible.[6]

Similarly, John Macquarrie mentions experience, revelation, scripture, tradition, and culture as sources for theology.[7] I do see the primacy of the Bible in Christian theological construction, but I do not consider it as the *only* source. Thus, it is clear to me that the starting point for a theology of mission cannot be the Bible as such if we take the view of theology as imaginative construction.

Even if one takes the Bible as the starting point, one is faced with another difficulty. The Bible is not a single book with a single understanding of what the mission of the church is. It is a library of sixty-six books written by a diversity of people in different periods of history. So to ask a library to begin a conversation on the theology of mission is quite a formidable task. Where and how we begin becomes difficult and complicated. The answer to this complexity, as it has often been worked out in Christian history, is to make particular texts or passages from the Bible the organizing center for this library of books. For example, the so-called Great Commission in the Gospel According to Matthew (28:16-20) was seen as the central text during the period of the modern missionary movement. Even today, there are several missiologists who would see that text as the definitive word for the understanding of mission. Mortimer Arias writes:

> The so-called Great Commission, from Matthew 28:16-20, has been the obligatory reference in the literature and the discussions on mission and evangelism during most of this century. . . . The first surprise is that the expression "the great commission" is not in the text. It is an editorial title supplied by the King James Version and those versions that follow the KJV precedent. In calling this passage "a commission" and "great," this title implies an interpretation and a value judgment.[8]

Another example is the way in which liberation theologians have used the "Nazareth Manifesto" in the Gospel According to Luke (4:16-20) as the "canon within the canon." As E. H. Scheffler writes:

> [Liberation theologians] draw upon the Exodus and prophetic traditions from the Old Testament. As far as the New Testament is concerned, a great interest has been shown in a political interpretation of the historical Jesus. The Gospel of Luke (as Gospel for the poor), and especially Luke 4:18 also feature prominently.[9]

Quite often, the discussion on mission undertaken by the "evangelicals" begins with the Matthean pericope,[10] whereas the "ecumenicals" have used the Lukan pericope as the organizing center for their theology of mission.[11] Therefore, anyone who intends to begin the discussion with the Bible as the starting point has to engage in a process of selection, and such selectivity alienates groups of Christians from the wider discussion rather than enabling a conversation.

Moreover, if we take seriously the concerns raised in the introduction — especially the desire to construct a theology of mission in conversation with partners both within and outside the boundaries of the Christian tradition — we simply cannot begin this theological construction with the Bible. In today's situation we are keenly aware of the multi-scriptural character of our context. Scriptures such as the Koran, the Bhagavad Gita, the Adi Granth, and others are accessible to English readers, and we are cognizant of the way in which those scriptures function as authoritative writings in each of those religious communities. This multi-scriptural awareness relativizes the Bible and helps us to see it as *one* among many sacred writings. The Bible is not a "public" book in the wider circle of discussion; it is a "private" book of a particular community of believers just as the other scriptures are to those of other religious communities.

Therefore, to begin a conversation on a theology of mission in the company of Christians, Jews, Muslims, Hindus, and others, one cannot start with the biblical materials. Let me offer an illustration here. Several times over the years I have led workshops in Madurai, India, on interreligious dialogue, with Christians, Hindus, Muslims, and others in attendance. On such occasions, I have often used the Constitution of India as the starting point for discussing interreligious dialogue because this was a document that all the participants acknowledged as authoritative for their political life. Therefore, one could begin the discussion by surveying the place of religion in the life of the nation as seen by the Constitution, and from there move to a discussion of the need for interreligious dialogue. The Bible is very different from the constitution of a particular nation. Whereas the constitution is a public document accepted by all within that nation as authoritative for political life and conduct, the Bible is not recognized in a similar way by the participants in our "circle of discussion."

Does this imply that the Bible is therefore no longer authoritative for Christian theological reflection? Not at all. In developing a specifically Christian theology of mission, one would invariably depend on the bib-

35

lical materials for articulation. The question here is: What is the most helpful starting point for constructing a theology of mission that takes the conversation with people of varying religious and ideological traditions as an important part of theological construction? The Bible fails to be such a helpful starting point. While we strongly affirm the centrality of the Bible within the Christian community—which in its early history adopted these writings as authoritative for its life and witness—the Bible has to take its place as one among many in a multi-scriptural context when we are engaging in a theological construction with inter-religious discussion at its heart.

Where then shall we begin? One may begin simply with the mission of the church, without immediately bringing the Bible into the discussion. But what does it mean to speak of the mission of "the church" in the wider circle of discussion? In so doing we immediately face three types of difficulties arising both from within and from outside the Christian community. First, within the Christian ecumenical family there is no single definitive understanding of "church." Anyone familiar with the worldwide ecumenical movement and the work of the World Council of Churches knows how difficult it is for the various churches in their denominational diversity to agree on any one definition of "the church." This is the primary reason that led to the "Toronto Statement" in which the World Council addressed the multiplicity of understandings and included statements such as the following:

> *The World Council cannot and should not be based on any one particular conception of the Church. It does not prejudge the ecclesiological problem. . . . Membership in the World Council of Churches does not imply that a church treats its own conception of the Church as merely relative.*[12]

The use of the word "church" in the singular has become highly problematic. One can speak only of "churches." An Eastern Orthodox student who was enrolled in my class on "The Church's Mission in a Pluralistic World" had been feeling uncomfortable with my use of the phrase "the church." One day halfway through the semester he took me aside and said, "Sir, I have a serious question. You use the phrase 'the church' so freely in this class as if there is something called 'the church' out there, so to speak. What do you really mean by the word 'church'? For me, the church primarily is a local congregation gathered for worship and Eucharist. Is that what you mean?" It is clear that a discussion of the mission of the church has to deal with the idea of church before going further. Or one may assume a working definition, in which case the participation of all in the circle of discussion becomes difficult. This is one reason why the World Council of Churches, right from its inception in 1948, has insisted that it is not in any way prejudging the issue of what is meant by the term "church."

The second difficulty comes from the fact that the word "church" is often linked with the so-called mainline Protestant, Roman Catholic, or Orthodox churches. This vision of the church has come under severe criticism from several quarters. The church has been seen as highly institutionalized, patriarchal, and bourgeois in character. In recent times women have been in the forefront in making such criticisms of the church. According to Rebecca Chopp, women "challenge the church as to whether or not it really is true to the Christian message and credible to contemporary human existence . . . [they aim to bring] the emancipatory transformation of the church, the emancipation of the church from its own patriarchal and dehumanizing practices, and the transformation of the church into a new nature and mission as ekklesia."[13] The church of the future is seen as "one expression of Christian dreams and desires, the anticipation of the unrealized possibilities of the present."[14] Like Chopp, more and more theologians are opting to use such phrases as "ecclesial communities," "ecclesia," and "ecclesial practices," while others prefer "women-church" rather than the phrase "the church."

In such a situation we will have to begin our discussions with a set of ecclesiological assumptions and then work toward an exposition of the mission of the church. But such an exercise leads to the third difficulty: It excludes from the conversation people who belong to other religious traditions. The church is an institution with its own rules of membership; those of other religions stand outside that institution and hence are not enthusiastic about discussing the mission of the church. Making "the church" our starting point leaves a large majority of humans (67 percent of the world's total population) outside the circle of discussion, because church is not the most inclusive category as far as humanity is concerned. The word "church" encompasses a divisive character and history. As one who comes from a multireligious and multicultural situation in which the church is a very small minority within India's majority Hindu and Muslim population, I am acutely aware of the divisive character of the word "church." To most people outside the church, it appears like a giant "corporation" with its educational, financial, religious, and cultic branches in place. It has failed to create and offer an open space for conversation. Therefore, one has to look for an alternative starting point.

Might the *missio Dei* (mission of God) function in this way? Since Karl Barth proposed the idea of *missio Dei* as the proper way of talking about the church's mission during the Brandenburg Missionary Conference in 1932, there has been a renewed interest in beginning the conversation on the mission of the church with the mission of God.[15] This has been due mainly to two reasons. First, following Barth's theological methodology, one may assert that theology proper would always begin with God, and therefore any talk about mission should be preceded by explicating the mission of God. In such a situation, a Christian cannot but begin with the very nature of God, as God has revealed Godself in Jesus the Christ. This would put the theology of mission squarely in the context of the doctrine of the Trinity. As one can see, we have begun our conversation with a heavily loaded agenda that includes most of the doctrines of the Christian church. How such a stance could facilitate an interreligious conversation on a theology of mission is highly questionable. Beginning the discussion with well-developed Christian theological assertions about God's nature and character already closes the doors on conversation before it begins.

My personal experiences in interreligious dialogue over the years confirm these fears. I have been a member of several interreligious dialogue groups that meet periodically at Madurai, South India, for conversation, discussion, and prayer. One is a group of Christians, Hindus, and Muslims who meet monthly for dialogue under the aegis of a program called "Religious Friends Circle" of the Tamilnadu Theological Seminary. Another is a smaller group of Christian theologians and Saivite philosophers. The Saivites are those Hindus who name Ultimate Reality as Siva and possess a well-developed scriptural and philosophical tradition in the Tamil language. This group meets in one another's homes for dialogue and prayer. The third is a group of people who, while belonging to various religious traditions, appreciate the teachings of Mahatma Gandhi. This group meets periodically for workshops on interreligious dialogue and gathers every Friday evening for *Sarvasamaya pirarthanai* (the prayer of all religions) on the lawn in front of the Gandhi Museum in Madurai.

In each of these groups I have found that one cannot possibly enter into serious and constructive dialogue on mission with an *a priori* definition of mission as *missio Dei*. An appropriate theology, relevant and meaningful to our context today, instead must emerge out of the conversation itself. Of course, this does not mean that one enters the dialogue with no prior commitments. All partners bring their commitments and convictions to bear on the conversation itself. But beginning the conversation with *missio Dei* already forecloses the discussion and defines the direction of the process in predetermined forms. This is more so because there is a variety of understandings of God within the circle of discussion. The word "God" in the English language has its own distinctive meanings derived mainly from the Christian tradition. Other religious traditions use terms such as Brahman, Allah, Yahweh, Siva, Great Spirit, and others, all of which carry unique significations for one's view of God. Therefore, the concept of *missio Dei* does not enable the conversation; it merely begs the question and stunts the conversation.

Second, some would see *missio Dei* as a helpful starting point because of the inclusive nature of the word "God." If God, in the English language, stands for the ultimate context of all that is, all that lives, and all that has being, then what could be more inclusive than "God"? Would not the very nature of God include all in the circle of discussion? Can we not revise Anselm's words and say that God is "that than which nothing more inclusive can be conceived"? This is a legitimate claim. God—the God who is the ground of all that is—does include all humans and everything nonhuman in all their diversity. It is possible thus to conceive of God in such totally and completely inclusive terms.

Within the missionary movement of the twentieth century, one can recognize this shift to the inclusive character of the concept of God. The idea of *missio Dei*—though initially put forward by Barth and others to center missiological thinking in the movement within the trinitarian God—was soon expanded to include God's activity in other places, persons, communities, and religions.[16] This, of course, was contrary to what Barth and like-minded theologians had envisaged in the primacy of *missio Dei*. According to this view, "the *missio Dei* is God's activity, which embraces both the church and the world, and in which the church may be privileged to participate."[17] Thus a wider understanding of *missio Dei* could lead to an inclusive circle of discussion.

While it is possible to conceive of God in such inclusive terms, the concept of God has not always functioned that way in human history. Since the known beginnings of human history, a sizable part of humanity has understood and lived out its existence without any reference to the idea of "God." If we are really keen on including so-called secular people in our circle of discussion, we cannot begin our conversation with *missio Dei*. For many of these persons, the way in which the *missio Dei* has been articulated and practiced by religious people is precisely the reason for their disillusionment with the idea of God. At the same time, these persons do not lack a sense of mission. For instance, those who are guided by Marxist ideologies live their lives with a great sense of missionary vocation—that of ushering in a classless society.[18] But they adopt a thoroughly atheistic position in terms of religious beliefs. Similarly, secular humanists operate with a keen sense of the need to "humanize" society, politics, and life as a whole. So while these persons are willing to engage in a conversation about mission, they are excluded from the circle of conversation right from the very beginning if *missio Dei* is the starting point. Moreover, there are religious traditions, such as Vedanta and certain forms of Buddhism, that do not operate with a theistic view of the universe. For them the concept of God does not enable a conversation on mission.

What I have proposed so far may sound problematic. One may wonder how one could ever envisage a Christian theology of mission without the Bible, the idea of "the church," and the *missio Dei*. What we are discussing here is a methodology that takes seriously the possibility of conversation among people from various religious and nonreligious traditions as the locus for articulating a theology of mission. Such a methodology demands that we open the conversation with the greatest number of persons in today's world as potential participants. As I mentioned in the introduction, the postmodern condition has given us a seriousness about conversation and an intense desire to engage in it. So far I have argued that we cannot begin the conversation with either the biblical views of mission, the mission of the church as such, or the *missio Dei*.

Are there other ways of beginning the conversation? One possibility is to begin with the idea of the mission of humanity. Let's call it *missio humanitatis*. The word "humanity" does include all human beings, irrespective of either their faith in God or their membership in any religious community. But here again we face a difficulty. Although all humans can be dialogically engaged in discussing the mission of humanity, our understanding of what it means to be human is varied and sometimes even contradictory. How can we proceed with a discussion of the mission of humanity when we do not agree on a common view of what it means to be human? Some may suggest that we look for a "universal" or "essential" understanding of what it means to be human and proceed from this foundation. As Gordon Kaufman notes:

> Some suggest we should attempt to overcome our traditional parochialism by moving to what they claim is a "universally human" position, one that penetrates beneath all the "accidental" and "historical" differences among humans and their religions to some supposed "essential oneness" we all share. . . . But there really is no such universally human position available to us; every religious (or secular) understanding and way of life we might uncover is a *particular* one.[19]

Although the meaning of "the mission of humanity" cannot be fixed by an essentialist definition of the human, there are, however, resources that can help us to understand and develop an appropriate meaning for this term—one larger than the meanings held by the church in the past. Let me suggest three such resources.

First, the fact that people *are* in fact engaging in conversation across religious and ideological boundaries over issues that affect humanity as a whole gives us confidence that we can engage in a conversation on the mission of humanity even given the variety of understandings of what it means to be human. Every meeting of the Parent-Teacher Association in our schools, every town hall meeting, each legislative session, and even our ordinary conversations with people of other religious and secular traditions are evidences that we already are engaged in a conversation on the mission of humanity. Such conversations may not be articulating this mission in the same way as I am attempting here. But the conversation does go on in our communities and neighborhoods.

Second, the word "mission," as I mentioned previously, is not the private property of Christian discourse. It is a word in the English language and thus part of our normal day-to-day usage. "Mission" is a public word. For example, corporations and other institutions are formulating "mission statements" for their organizations, and the catalogue of the place where I teach opens with a "mission statement."

When I visited a friend staying at a La Quinta Inn, I was greeted by a big and nicely framed mission statement hanging on the wall at the receptionist's desk! That statement outlined the mission of La Quinta Inn. "Mission" is an ordinary, everyday word.

In earlier times, especially in countries like India, the word "mission" was closely and often solely associated with the work of the Christian missionaries. But today the word is appropriated and used by Hindus themselves in naming such institutions as Hindu Mission Hospital and so on. As we have already seen, the word "mission" is not a peculiarly religious term. National governments talk about their political mission, trade missions, and peace missions. The movie and television industries use this word in all possible ways, including the activity of the fictional agent James Bond 007. Thus, the public character of the word "mission" makes it possible for us to engage in a discussion about the idea of *missio humanitatis* in a larger human context.

Philosophers and theologians have reminded us of the value of the "ordinariness" of our language. Placing the writings of Wittgenstein and Kaufman side by side, Alec Irwin shows how both thinkers have given central attention to the notions of "the ordinary" and "ordinariness." He writes:

> Finding words distorted—lost and exiled—by the uses to which they are put in philosophy, Wittgenstein seeks to "bring [them] back" to the ordinary contexts, the everyday patterns of speech and behavior in which they had their "original home." . . . Similarly, Kaufman affirms that, in theology, specialists' habit of isolating religious or theological uses of words from the wider, common language in which all such uses are embedded leads to "truncated and one-sided interpretations" of theological symbols.[20]

If we follow the argument here, it is quite viable to engage in a conversation on the mission of humanity, given the "ordinariness" of the words "mission" and "humanity."

Third, if one seriously takes into account the emerging "historical consciousness" that is affecting almost all human communities and nations across the world, then one may be emboldened to assert a few basic affirmations about the nature of the human from a historicist perspective. By "historical consciousness" I mean an intense and intentional awareness that human beings are fundamentally historical creatures who, although they create their own historical traditions and cultural expressions, are significantly shaped and oriented by the same history and culture. This consciousness also includes a forthright recognition that humans create these traditions in diverse ways. Even though the kind of historical consciousness to which I refer here grew out of the Western theological, philosophical, and scientific traditions, we now live in a period when such consciousness has come to pervade larger and larger portions of humanity. For example, the sociopolitical life of India, both during and after the struggle for independence, bears ample witness to the emergence of historical consciousness in Indian society and politics. More recently, the Hindu's rediscovery of the "history" of the town of Ayodhya as the birthplace of Rama (an incarnation of God) and of the subsequent events that led to the destruction of the mosque in that town illustrate this historical consciousness. The liberalization of India's economy in recent years is yet another illustration of this emergence. The democratization of Eastern Europe, the Tamil independence struggle in Sri Lanka, and other such movements illustrate the development of historical consciousness on a global level. The arrival of cable TV, the Internet, and other modes of communication has strengthened this global historical perspective.

Therefore, what I offer here is a set of affirmations about the human that help us to situate and account for the plurality of understandings of what it means to be human. I am not developing these affirmations in detail; rather, I offer them as a way to recognize plurality and thus move out of the bottleneck created by it to a possibility for conversation on *missio humanitatis*.[21] The issue at this point is this: Is it possible to engage in a conversation on *missio humanitatis*, given the plurality of understandings? The three affirmations that I offer here will help us to answer this question in the affirmative.

First, humans are self-conscious beings. This simply means that there is an internal relation in every human being, wherein the self is able to relate to its own self. This internal relation can also be called reflexive consciousness. Such a reflexive consciousness is not merely something that humans possess; it is constitutive of what it means to be human. Our being human is constituted by the understanding of the human that we hold. Defending the original character of self-consciousness against naturalistic reductionism, Manfred Frank names it as our "epistemic familiarity with ourselves" and goes on to explain it as constitutive of what it means to be human.[22] Modern scientific research on primates is more and more convinced that self-consciousness is not totally peculiar to humans alone. Other primates may have traces of such self-consciousness. My assertion, however, is simply that humans possess reflexive consciousness and it is a constitutive part of what it means to be human. Different religious and theological traditions may name this consciousness differently. One may name it "soul," *"jiva," "atman,"* and the like. In each of these cases, however, humans hold these ideas about themselves, and these ideas shape the way they think and live in the world.

Second, humans are historical beings. By historicity I mean that creativity by which humans transcend the limitations of time and space in order to create history. In turn they are shaped and constituted by that history. In other words, historicity includes both the creativity in human relations and in relation to the world and a recognition that one is shaped by the traditions within which one is situated. Even when a particular religious tradition envisions "history" as an illusion, its vision is an expression of the historical creativity of the human and shapes and influences the way in which the people of that particular religious tradition live in the world. Although located in the natural and material world, humans can create artificial worlds of their own, such as those of religion, art, music, and culture, and in turn be influenced by them. As Kaufman writes:

> In and through this culture-creating activity . . . human life has become radically diverse in its manifestations and pluralistic in its most fundamental structures. . . . Humans, thus, have emerged from the strictly biological order into a cultural or spiritual order in which they are able (to some extent) to set their own goals, to create and serve new values and meanings, to give life forms which they themselves choose.[23]

Third, humans are ecological beings. They are part of a network of ecological interdependence. Humans are not disembodied historical spirits; they are "the dust of the earth" and creatures of the planet earth. This ecological dependence is something that constitutes the human and provides the framework for a variety of expressions and ways of being human. One can see how geography and history are constitutive elements in the human. Given the disastrous and demonic consequences of an undue emphasis on the history-making character of the human, which leads to ecological imbalance in the world of nature, there is an increasing desire among all religious communities and secular traditions to reiterate the ecological dependence of the human.

In describing the combination of cultural creativity and ecology in the human, Kaufman uses the helpful phrase "biohistorical beings." Humans are biohistorical beings who, while having their feet solidly on the ground of this planet earth and the wider ecosystem, are able to travel far and wide into worlds of their own, creating beauty and order.

What I have shown through these affirmations is simply this: While there is, in fact, a multiplicity of understandings of the human, we can recognize the interconnectedness of these differing views at the level of self-consciousness, historicity, and ecological interdependence. Such a recognition makes it possible to engage in a conversation toward developing a common understanding of *missio humanitatis*. Together with the public character of the word "mission" and the very fact of ongoing conversations on *missio humanitatis* in our own social, political, and communal settings, one can argue that it is possible to engage in a conversation on the mission of humanity.

Once we have decided to start our theological construction with a conversation on the mission of humanity, the question becomes: What is *missio humanitatis*? To answer this question, we need to return to the word "mission" in its root-meaning and put forward some possible ways in which one may explicate this term within the framework of the understanding of human reflexivity, historicity, and ecological interdependence. In the next chapter I will suggest "responsibility," "solidarity," and "mutuality" as concepts that may aid us in putting forward a picture of what *missio humanitatis* may look like.

2

Missio Humanitatis

So far I have argued that one of the best ways to engage in the construction of a theology of mission is to begin a conversation on the idea of *missio humanitatis* with both Christians and people of other religious and secular persuasions. It is possible to engage one another in this discussion given the public character of the word "mission" and the "biohistorical" character of the human. How then shall we go about organizing our thoughts on the mission of humanity?

Let us begin with the word "mission" itself. In the history of Christianity, "mission" has come to signify several things. David Bosch lists eight different meanings.[1] One set of meanings is related to the sending and receiving of Christian missionaries from one particular region of the world to another. This set includes, first, the act of sending itself. This meaning is closest to the literal meaning of the term. "Mission" means "being sent." It comes from a Latin root word signifying being sent. Of course, in the Christian usage of that term, the New Testament Greek term *apostello*, which means "to send," has been significantly influential in shaping the meaning of the term "mission." Second, mission refers to the work of the missionaries. Sentences like "You are sent on a mission" or "This is our mission" refer to that particular meaning. Third, the organization that sends these missionaries is called the Mission. For example, the people in my ancestral village used to refer to themselves as belonging to the SPG Mission (The Society for the Propagation of the Gospel of the Church of England) and the people in the neighboring village as belonging to the CMS Mission (Church Missionary Society of the Church of England). "Mission" referred to the agency or organization that recruited, sent, and supported missionaries. Fourth, the region or the land where the missionaries are engaged in is "mission." Another set of meanings is related to places. Sometimes, for example, when people use the word "mission" they mean that part of the world that has not yet been "evangelized." Other times, one may mean the central place from which the missionaries operate in a particular region. Yet another meaning is the local congregation that has not yet become an autonomous church but is under the supervisory control of the missionaries. As we can see, then, in the historical Christian tradition the word "mission" has had a variety of meanings.

As we saw in chapter 1, when we move out of ecclesial history and look at the way "mission" is used in the wider society, we again encounter a variety of meanings. For example, *Webster's Third New International Dictionary* lists several meanings, which include (a) "a group of persons sent to a foreign country to conduct diplomatic or political negotiations"; (b) "a team of military specialists sent to a foreign country to assist in the training of its armed forces"; (c) "a specific task with which a person or group is charged"; (d) "the chief function or responsibility of an organization or institution"; and (e) "a continuing task or responsibility that one is destined or fitted to do or specially called upon to undertake."

When one looks carefully at this wide variety of meanings, two factors stand out. Mission has to do with "sending" and "going." In a way, the literal meaning of the term "mission"—namely, "being sent"—is kept intact in all these different understandings. Mission is "being-sent-ness" or "going-forth-ness." This "sent-ness" is not seen in spatial terms. It is rather a quality of being. In that sense, it is a task; it is a responsibility. The nature of the task may not be the same in all instances, but mission is a task. Second, mission is something that happens in a network of relations. It may be a relation between the missionaries and the people in a particular region of the world, or it may be that of the military specialists and the armed forces. Mission is thus a relational term. It is not something an individual does in his or her solitude. Mission is carried out in the matrix of human relationships; it is a communal affair.

Having defined "mission" in this twofold manner, we need to ask ourselves now: What is the mission of humanity? I wish to attempt an answer to this question by organizing the idea of *missio humanitatis* around three terms or concepts, namely, *responsibility*, *solidarity*, and *mutuality*. These three terms in no way exhaust or fully define the meaning of mission, either Christian or otherwise. This is simply my way of explicating the idea of mission in relation to *missio humanitatis*. These terms are offered as heuristic devices to organize our thoughts on and around *missio humanitatis*.

One may ask at this point whether the very choice of the terms *responsibility*, *solidarity*, and *mutuality* is already informed by a Christian bias in the understanding of the mission of humanity. I need to answer this query with a "yes" and a "no." I am a Christian theologian, and when I suggest words or concepts to think through the idea of mission, I am already informed heavily by the long tradition of Christian theological and missiological thinking. In this sense, the choice of the three terms is shaped by a Christian bias. But at the same time I would argue that my point of departure for discussing the idea of *missio humanitatis* is precisely the idea of "responsibility" that is already embedded in the popular meaning of the term "mission." The word "responsibility," in its formal sense, is not peculiarly Christian. Therefore I am offering these three terms in their formal sense rather than in any concrete material sense. Moreover, while it is true that a Christian theologian cannot at any given moment suspend all Christian perspectives and look at a theological issue in a vacuum, it is possible, in a setting of multireligious and multicultural conversation, to relativize one's particular stance for a time and work toward a more inclusive understanding of mission. This kind of relativizing is not only possible, it is also necessary in a setting of conversation. Furthermore, bringing these three terms into the discussion is only an initial step in the constructing of a theology of mission. It is not, by any means, the final word on mission. As I mentioned earlier, these three terms function simply as heuristic devices for a discussion of *missio humanitatis*.

Responsibility

Taking our point of departure from the primary meaning of the word "mission" both within and outside the *ecclesia*, we may describe the *missio humanitatis*—that is, the nature of the "being-sent-ness" of the human—as an act of responsibility. One of the monumental works on the idea of responsibility in this century is H. Richard Niebuhr's slim but profound volume titled *The Responsible Self: An Essay in Christian Moral Philosophy.*[2] I am aware that Niebuhr used the concept of responsibility to explicate the ethical dimension of human life. But I find his discussion very appropriate for our understanding of the mission of humanity as well. Gordon Kaufman, building on Niebuhr's work, has also described human moral agency in terms of responsibility.[3]

Niebuhr begins his discussion on the meaning of responsibility by noting how this word in recent times has come to the forefront in describing human existence. Though the idea of responsibility as a way of symbolizing human existence has prefigured in the writings of Aristotle and others, it has gained much more significance in the twentieth century.[4] Niebuhr elaborates four distinct elements within the idea of responsibility. The first is the concept of *response*. Niebuhr writes: "All action, we now say, including what we rather indeterminately call moral action is response to action upon us."[5]

But second, the response we are referring to here is not a response in a vacuum. It is executed in the context of our own interpretation of what has been an action upon us. Drawing upon everyday instances of our responses to actions upon us, Niebuhr argues that the second element in responsibility is "not only responsive action but responsive in accordance with our *interpretation* of the question to which the answer is being given." "What is going on?" is a question prior to the question "What shall I do?" The third element in responsibility, for Niebuhr, is the idea of *accountability*. He compares our action to "a statement in a dialogue" and sees accountability as a significant part of the conversation that goes on between the self and the world in every action.[6] The fourth element in the idea of responsibility is what Niebuhr calls *social solidarity*. Interpretation and accountability make sense only in a community of agents and in the context of "a continuing discourse or interaction among beings forming a continuing society."[7]

In the context of Christian ethics, William Schweiker puts forward three types of theories of responsibility: agential, social, and dialogical.[8] The primary focus of agential theories of responsibility is the acting agent himself or herself. If an agent causes a particular thing to happen, then he or she is responsible for that event. Social theories of responsibility, according to Schweiker, "focus on social roles, vocations, stations, and thus communal unity."[9] Finally, "dialogical theories of responsibility center on the event of encounter between an agent and some 'other.' "[10] Schweiker places Niebuhr's view with the third of these theories.

It is not necessary, for our purposes here, to go into a detailed discussion of the ideas of responsibility propounded by Niebuhr, Kaufman, or Schweiker. Yet I do want to show the relevance and usefulness of the "dialogical" interpretation of responsibility for our own elaboration of the idea of *missio humanitatis*. The mission of humans—that is, the "being-sent-ness" or the "going-forth-ness" of the human—can be viewed as the response of the human to the other. The other here includes other humans, animals, plants, trees, and all that is around us. We as humans respond to all that goes on around us. We respond to persons, things, events, natural phenomena, and so forth as they impinge upon us. One may call human existence a "missionary" mode of existence; that is, we "go forth" and respond to all that is around us.

This "going-forth-ness" is not simply a one-way street. It also involves a returning-to-ourselves through the interpretation of persons, things, and events. The two-way character of our "mission" is what is meant by Niebuhr's way of putting response and interpretation as two sides of the same coin. One cannot exist without the other. This somewhat circular movement of response and interpretation, in turn, evolves into a sense of accountability. In responding to other individuals, things, and events, we come to see ourselves as accountable to ourselves, others, and the wider context of human existence. In this manner, one may say that the mission of humanity is simply the act of taking responsibility.

Such a "dialogical" view of responsibility fits very well with the three basic assumptions that I made in the previous chapter with regard to the nature of the human. I pointed out that the self-conscious, historical, and ecological character of the human is that which gives rise to manifold understandings of what it means to be human and also provides a framework for engaging in a conversation on the mission of humanity. In revisiting those assumptions, one can see how a dialogical view of responsibility fits with them. In other words, our picture of the human as a self-conscious, historical, and ecological being can be filled out, to some extent, by this concept of responsibility. I would argue that the very element of self-consciousness in the human is a missionary mode of being human. Self-consciousness in itself is a dialogue. It is a conversation within myself, a way of responding to the other "me." I respond to the other within me with an interpretation. Such an interpretation of oneself by one's own self is what guides one's responses to events and things and what makes one accountable and responsible. In this sense, self-consciousness is one's mission to oneself—a mission expressed in the relation of the self to its own self. A good illustration of this "missionary" character of the human is the very task of telling or writing one's autobiography. Humans tell and retell their life stories. Every time one's autobiography is either narrated or written, one is responding to and interpreting all that has gone on around oneself. In that process one expresses accountability and responsibility for one's own life story.

If we take into account both the cultural-creativity and the ecological dependence of the human, we can again see how these realities are acts of responsibility in the dialogical sense of the term. The historical and ecological dimensions of human existence portray our connectedness to history, culture, and the material world. We live in these worlds of culture, history, and ecology, and we respond to these worlds. In this process of responding to the worlds of culture and ecology, we become accountable. To the extent that our responses are also shaped by our ideas of these worlds, we become accountable not simply for our ideas and responses but also to and for that to which we are connected as "biohistorical" beings. In this sense our connectedness with the cultural and ecological world in which we live constitutes our mission of responsibility to and for that world. Let me offer an illustration here. Whenever I attend a classical music concert in South India, I find myself responding to the music through the acts of listening to it, interpreting it, and enjoying it. At the same time, I find within me a wellspring of responsibility emerging. I want to make sure that the performer has a good audience. I nod my head and offer him or her symbolic gestures of appreciation and affirmation. In relating to the world of culture and ecology, we express our responsibility in a variety of ways as well.

To sum up our discussion on responsibility, we are beings who by the very structure of our existence are in a "missionary" mode of existence. We are those who go forth from ourselves and back to ourselves in our reflexive consciousness, interpret ourselves, and with a sense of accountability take responsibility for ourselves and our actions. We are those who go forth from ourselves to others in our cultural creativity, interpret the world of peoples and cultures around us, and with a sense of accountability take responsibility for others and our world. We are also those who go forth from ourselves to the natural world around us, interpret it, and take responsibility for it. Thus the mission of humanity is to take responsibility for ourselves, others, and the world. If we place here the well-known question of Cain's in the biblical story—"Am I my brother's (or sister's) keeper?"—we will definitely say "Yes." That is what *missio humanitatis* is all about.

Solidarity

In explaining the concept of responsibility as a way of explicating the mission of humanity, I have focused mostly on the first three elements of responsibility as outlined by Niebuhr, namely, response, interpretation, and accountability. The fourth element is what Niebuhr calls social solidarity, a concept to which he devotes an entire chapter.[11]

For Niebuhr, the idea of solidarity is linked to the need for "continuing discourse or interaction among beings forming a continuing society." In elaborating this idea he brings in the concept of I-Thou relations and I-You relations. As he writes: "The social self exists in responses neither to atomic other beings nor to a generalized other or impartial spectator but to others who as Thous are members of a group in whose interactions constancies are present in such a way that the self can interpret present and anticipate future action upon it."[12] He then goes on to describe how the ecological framework of the human provides the third element of the I-Thou relationality. While I fully agree with Niebuhr's explication of the idea of social solidarity, I want to bring the idea of solidarity into the discussion of the mission of humanity from a different angle.

While the word "responsibility" is dialogical in character, it also has the danger of implying that it is something *we* do for others: *we* take responsibility *for* others. This is a problematic element in responsibility. Human history bears ample evidence of the tragedy of humans' taking responsibility *for* others. Through the ages we have seen individuals, groups, and nations arrogating to themselves responsibility for the destiny of their neighbors. Such an assumption of *missio humanitatis* has often resulted in disastrous and highly oppressive consequences. For example, throughout human history men have assumed that they are "responsible" for women. The Christian scriptures talk about men-women relationships in this manner. Paul, writing to the Christians at Corinth, says: "The women should keep silence in the churches. For they are not permitted to speak, but should be subordinate, as even the law says. If there is anything they desire to know, let them ask their husbands at home" (1 Cor. 14:34-35 RSV). One finds a similar sentiment expressed in the law books of the Hindu religious tradition. *The Laws of Manu* state: "In childhood a female must be subject to her father, in youth to her husband, when her lord is dead to her sons; a woman should never be independent."[13]

Similarly, the two World Wars of this century bear witness to the demonic distortion of human responsibility. The Nazis, in one sense, assumed "responsibility" for the well-being of the world in their own terms, and that assumption led to tragic and destructive consequences. The scandalous history of relations between the Anglo-Americans and African Americans in the United States is another example of this demonic sense of responsibility. The relation between the upper caste groups and the so-called untouchables in India is yet another case of such an atrocious sense of responsibility. This has been true of the relations between the oppressors and the oppressed—whether economically, politically, culturally, or socially—throughout the world.

Moreover, the current ecological crisis is a supreme example of the kind of *missio humanitatis* that has led humans to take oppressive responsibility for nature, and by so doing, to move the planet to the brink of an ecological disaster. The very sustaining context of human and other life is at stake in this kind of responsibility. We respond to nature with our own interpretation of nature as an "it" and exploit its resources, totally unmindful of the ecological imbalance such an act of "responsibility" can create.

Thus, we cannot define the mission of humanity in terms of responsibility alone. If the mission of humanity is an *act* of responsibility, it must be done in a *mode* of solidarity. Response and responsibility do not always mean an "over-against-ness"; rather, they involve much more a "being-with-ness." Since the advent of liberation theologies in various religious traditions, the word "solidarity" has come to the forefront of discussion. Solidarity stands for relationships between humans and others that respect the distinctiveness of each person, the interweaving of structural relations, and a willingness to work *with* and *alongside* the other. In describing the importance of distinction in the idea of solidarity, Ruy O. Costa writes:

> Solidarity presumes distinction. . . . Canaries will be happy with their gift of poetry; peacocks will be proud of their gift of colors; and they will not . . . conclude that everybody has to become a copy of themselves. Solidarity at this level means renouncing all interference in one another's projects. . . . In practice, this is a solidarity of non-interference.[14]

While this is true of and important for our understanding of solidarity, the idea of accountability is very strong in the idea of solidarity. As Beverly Harrison has pointed out, solidarity "is accountability, and accountability means being vulnerable" and being changed by the other. Such solidarity welcomes the other's "capacity to critique and alter our reality."[15] As we noted earlier, accountability is a vital element in the idea of responsibility, and by adding the word "solidarity" to responsibility we strengthen the element of accountability. Ada Maria Isasi-Diaz considers solidarity as the way to express the love of one's neighbor in contemporary times.[16] Solidarity, she argues, keenly recognizes the interconnectedness of human life. She writes: "Solidarity is *not* a matter of agreeing with, of being supportive of, of liking, or of being inspired by, the cause of a group of people. . . . Solidarity has to do with understanding the interconnections among issues and the cohesiveness that needs to exist among the communities of struggle."[17]

As I mentioned earlier, responsibility is not simply a matter of "over-against-ness." It is an expression of "being-with-ness," and that is what we mean by an act of responsibility that is exercised in a mode of solidarity. Our act of being responsible to and for all that is around us has to be coupled with a mode of being in solidarity. Without a sense of solidarity, with both other humans and nature, there is no creative responsibility, individual or social.

If we recall our description in the previous chapter of humanity as self-conscious, historical, and ecological, we can see the relevance of the idea of solidarity to such a view of the human. The interconnectedness of humans to one another and the interdependence of humans and other beings on this planet places humans in a setting of solidarity. The very "going-forth-ness" of the human is possible only in a situation of interpersonal relations, social networks of relationships, and close connections with the ecological moorings of human life. Thus the missionary character of the human does involve an expression of solidarity. Now we are in a position to define the mission of humanity as being in solidarity with others in the acting out of one's responsibility. In other words, *missio humanitatis* is both responsibility and solidarity.

Mutuality

The phrase *missio humanitatis* in itself suggests that mission is common to all humans. It universalizes the concept of mission. All humans have a mission to accomplish in terms of responsibility and solidarity. If all humans are self-conscious, historical, and ecological beings, then all are necessarily "missionary" beings—namely, beings who experience a "being-sent-ness" or a "going-forth-ness" resulting from their being human. It becomes a constitutive part of their being human. We need, however, to reiterate and strengthen this aspect of inclusivity and universality by bringing a third element into the idea of *missio humanitatis:* mutuality.

The idea of mutuality has become prominent in the writings of feminist thinkers. Darlene Ehinger discusses the idea of mutuality as it surfaces in the writings of Carol Gilligan and says:

> Most feminist ethicists recognize and accept the notion of connectiveness as a foundational concept in articulating a social ethic. We are born into this world as connected selves. Our connection to others is prior to our individual autonomy and our freedom. Our ethical response is always between self and others.[18]

Theologians of various persuasions and traditions have incorporated the idea of mutuality into their discussions of human relationality. For example, James W. Fowler, in laying out the different stages of faith, brings in the idea of mutuality at the very initial stage of faith. The formation of our images of God are, for him, "composed from our first experiences of *mutuality,* in which we form the rudimentary awareness of self as separate from and dependent upon the immensely powerful others."[19]

Leonard Swidler addresses the question of mutuality from the standpoint of epistemology and lists four different ways in which truth has been deabsolutized in our times.[20] The "historicizing of truth," "the sociology of knowledge," "the limitations of language," and Hans-Georg Gadamer's view of truth as interpreted truth have all contributed to the deabsolutizing of truth and have made mutuality a basic necessity for today's discourse. He further uncovers the psychological elements in the idea of mutuality through the writings of Fowler, Gilligan, and others, and goes on to reiterate the importance of mutuality in human relations.

For our purposes here, mutuality means that humans have a mission to one another. Mission is possible only in a spirit of mutuality in the sphere of interhuman relations. There are no longer "missioners" and the "missioned." All are missionaries in a relationship of mutuality. This fact is highly significant if we take seriously the multireligious and pluralistic character of the context in which we attempt to articulate the mission of humanity, because only by recognizing this mutuality can there be an "open marketplace of human experience and ideas" in which we can learn from each other.

History proves that we have not always appreciated the mode of mutuality in our relations. Humans have related to each other in an I-It relationship rather than an I-Thou relationship. The tragic history of slavery bears ample witness to this. Similarly, the way in which various societies have organized themselves in the past and continue to do so is indicative of this lack of mutuality. Hierarchical patterns of human relations reflect such lack of mutuality. In the history of Christian missionary movements of the last three centuries, for example, one can detect this problem. The very employment of the term "mission field" to denote a group of people or nations is symptomatic of the kind of I-It relationship the missionary enterprise had entailed. This particular problem has also been quite apparent in the way humans have exploited nature and natural resources for our own greedy desires of consumption. The world of nature has been viewed as an "It" to be subdued and dominated. Such a view of nonmutual relations with nature has led to disastrous consequences of ecological imbalance. Environmental protection is absolutely crucial for our continued existence on this planet, and this fact calls for a spirit of mutuality in our relation with nature. Thus, *missio humanitatis*, if it is to be a responsible vision, must include a spirit of mutuality both in our interhuman relations and in our relation to the world of nature.

Our construction of a theology of mission for our times began with an affirmation that conversation should be the method and source of our articulation. This means that dialogue and interchange of ideas become extremely important. Viewing mission as an exercise in mutuality assists us in maintaining the priority of conversation throughout our exploration. Without mutuality, *both* the mission of humanity *and* our articulation of that mission sink into parallel monologues, never meeting at any point.

A View of *Missio Humanitatis*

What I have done so far is present a set of terms/concepts by which one may engage in a conversation on the mission of humanity. According to this vision, *the mission of humanity is an act of taking responsibility, in a mode of solidarity, shot through with a spirit of mutuality.* This, I believe, expresses the way one can view the "going-forth-ness" of the human. I would like to close this discussion with three important observations. First, what I have outlined so far is *not* a vision of *missio humanitatis* that all humans and communities of humans will readily accept or that I wish they would readily accept. What I have provided here is a "language" to engage in a conversation about the mission of humanity. "What are we to do as humans?" is the question here, and an answer is offered in the most formal sense. We need to remind ourselves that the task we set out to do is not to construct a vision of *missio humanitatis* for its own sake. If that were our goal, we would have to continue this conversation in such a way that, through dialogue and interchange with others, we might arrive at a paradigm of *missio humanitatis* that we all could affirm as our common mission irrespective of our religious, ideological, and cultural differences. But our task is much more modest than that. It is to construct a *Christian theology* of mission, for which task the vision of a mission of humanity serves both as a heuristic device and as framework for conversation toward a relevant theology of mission.

Second, so far I have offered form and content to the concept of the mission of humanity as seen from a "historicist" perspective—a perspective that takes seriously the self-conscious, biohistorical, and ecological character of the human. In this process, we have not addressed the concept of God at all. That means that our exercise thus far has not yet moved to a level of *theological* exploration. As any theologian of mission would rightly demand, only when we allow the concept of God to "preside over" our discussion of mission do we begin to move toward a *theology* of mission.

Third, as we step into this "theological" dimension of our project, we need to recognize what is happening to our circle of dialogue partners. When we bring the word "God" into a discussion of mission, we are making a point of departure, which means that some of our dialogue partners may begin to see themselves as being outside the circle of discussion. The nontheists of the world are tempted to say good-bye to us. Even the theists face a difficulty in continuing the conversation, because none of us speaks of God in a vacuum. Our vision of God is shaped and formed by a particular religious and theological tradition. For example, we as Christian theologians cannot discuss a theology of mission as such but only a *Christian* theology of mission. Our understanding of *missio Dei* is normatively determined by our view of *missio Christi*. Therefore, the theists of religious traditions other than Christianity are in no way in a better position than the nontheists for continuing the conversation. Nevertheless, I believe that it is possible to continue the dialogue given the formal conceptual framework of the mission of humanity as I have outlined so far. Although the particular explications of responsibility, solidarity, and mutuality may vary according to the religious or secular tradition within which one undertakes them, it is still possible to sustain the conversation because of the concept of mutuality built into our view of *missio humanitatis*.

I had occasion to present these ideas about a possible theology of mission to a group of theological students in India. While they were highly appreciative of my efforts to engage in a wider conversation in the process of constructing such a theology of mission, they were very skeptical of sustaining the conversation with the other religious and secular partners once we introduce the concept of God in Christ. They were aware, on the one hand, that as Christian theologians their task is to talk of mission in light of God, Christ, and the church. But on the other hand, they were equally conscious that these categories become blocks to continuing the conversation. Interestingly, however, a Hindu philosopher present at the seminar maintained that as long as one operates within the framework of responsibility, solidarity, and mutuality, it still would be possible for a Hindu to continue in the conversation, even though a Hindu may bring his or her own particular understandings with regard to the elaboration of these basic concepts. This and other such experiences that I have had in multireligious gatherings have given me confidence in this process of conversation.

In the next chapter I will investigate how the three basic elements in the mission of humanity acquire a distinctive theological dimension as we move toward a Christian theology of mission.

3

Missio Ecclesiae

In the last chapter I outlined the three concepts which might be used to describe the mission of humanity—responsibility, solidarity, and mutuality—in a setting of conversation among people of various religious persuasions. Thus I defined *missio humanitatis* as the act of taking responsibility, in a mode of solidarity, shot through with a spirit of mutuality. Now, I move on to explicate a specifically *Christian* and *theological* view of mission. Though the kind of *missio humanitatis* that I have outlined may assist us in engaging in conversation with a wide variety of people, it does not satisfy fully the demands of a Christian theology of mission. It offers only a setting in which we may bring into view our specifically Christian theological interpretation.

The step we are taking now involves at least the following three moves. First of all, a theology of mission demands that we bring "God" into the discussion. As theologians are fond of saying, the proper business of theology is to talk about God. In this sense, all theology is God-talk. So a theological discussion of mission demands that our talk about mission be "presided over" and directed by our vision and understanding of God. In other words, *missio humanitatis* will have to be redefined or qualified by *missio Dei.* The leading question here will be: What is the mission of humans in light of the ongoing mission of God? Therefore, the step we are taking involves outlining the mission of God as the first move. But this move has to be accompanied simultaneously by a second one.

The second move is to talk about *missio Christi.* This move is necessary for two reasons. First, none of us talk about God in isolation from a particular religious or spiritual tradition/community. Our understanding of God is significantly shaped and influenced by the traditions and communities to which we belong. Therefore, as a theologian who stands within the Christian community of faith, my talk about God cannot help but be shaped by the theological category and symbol we name "Christ." Second, and much more important, "Christ" is a category that is normative for Christian theological reflection. In comparing and contrasting the manner in which Judaism, Islam, and Christianity have worked out their monotheistic beliefs, Gordon Kaufman has this to say:

> Christian faith, life, and theology are distinguished from these other two traditions by the addition of a fourth category [the other three being God, humanity, and world] — Christ — to the basic monotheistic framework of interpretation. This category, moreover, is just as important in defining and articulating the Christian world-picture as are the other three. . . . It is this category in particular, we could say, that distinguishes and defines a perspective as "Christian."[1]

The normative role of "Christ" in Christian theological articulation is what makes any theological reflection "Christian." This does not mean that there is *one* view of Christ that will function as the critical principle for Christian theology. In fact there are multiple visions of what the category and symbol "Christ" mean among those who claim allegiance to Jesus the Christ. Consequently, there will be a plurality of Christian theologies and multiple understandings of mission as well. Our project here, however, is to construct a Christian theology of mission.

Before I proceed to discuss the third move, let me digress for a moment. I would argue that bringing "God" and "Christ" into the articulation of a theology of mission really involves a vision of a God who is in mission. *Missio Dei* (mission of God) has been an important concept for missiological explorations within the ecclesial communities. But is God indeed in mission? If so, what does it mean to speak of God's being in mission? If we go back to our earlier definition of mission as going-forth-ness, one can see how the Christian theological tradition can rightly claim God to be in mission. This claim is sustained by two specific beliefs about God. First, at the very heart or inner self of God there is a journeying or going forth. The doctrine of the Trinity is a significant way in which the Christian faith has celebrated this idea. God goes forth as "three persons in one." The classical language which speaks of the members of the Trinity in "procession" is definitely indicative of the inner missionary character of God. K. C. Sen, a Hindu theologian who had a keen insight into Christian theological viewpoints, names the three members of the Trinity thus: "the Still God, the Journeying God, the Returning God."[2]

Second, God is also portrayed as One who is going forth toward all creation. The doctrine of the Incarnation is concerned precisely with the explication of the idea of God's going forth toward the world. K. C. Sen describes this movement again in trinitarian terms. He writes: "God descends and touches one end of the base of humanity, then running all along the base permeates the world, and then by the power of the Holy Ghost drags up regenerated humanity to Himself. Divinity coming down to humanity is the Son; Divinity carrying up humanity to heaven is the Holy Ghost."[3]

Thus we can see that the picture of God that emerges in the Christian theological tradition is a God who is in mission — going forth within God's own self, and going forth toward the world for its redemption and fulfillment. Therefore, what we are attempting is to reconstruct the three leading concepts — responsibility, solidarity, and mutuality — in light of this "missionary" God.

Let me return to the earlier line of argument and discuss the third step in the definition of a *Christian* theology of mission: to describe *missio ecclesiae*, the mission of the church. A Christian theology of mission is ultimately concerned with articulating how the church ought to understand its mission in the world in light of this conversation on *missio humanitatis*. Therefore, to redefine responsibility, solidarity, and mutuality from a Christian theological angle is to articulate the mission of the church. I am fully aware that using the term "church" at this point in our project raises more questions than answers. Hence the word "church" here is used in the broadest sense to include any and all intentional communities of faith that take the Christ-event (however various their interpretations of it) as the center for their formation and orientation. For this reason some may prefer the term *ecclesial communities* to *church* in this context.

As we step into the Christian theological discussion, I propose that we understand the mission of ecclesial communities as *cruciform responsibility, liberative solidarity,* and *eschatological mutuality.*

Cruciform Responsibility

When we place the concept of responsibility under the concept of God in the Christian tradition, we must introduce several nuances and implications into the discussion of responsibility. God, in the Christian tradition, has always been referred to as the Creator. The Hebrew Bible opens with the story of God's creation of the world and all its inhabitants. "In the beginning God created the heavens and the earth" (Gen. 1:1 RSV). This theme is carried throughout the Hebrew Bible and persists in the New Testament as well. God speaks thus through the prophet Isaiah: "I am He, I am the first, and I am the last. My hand laid the foundation of the earth, and my right hand spread out the heavens" (Isa. 48:12-13 RSV). One recognizes the same idea expressed in the teachings of Jesus. The preaching of the apostles, as recorded in the Acts of the Apostles, continues the same tradition (see Acts 14:15-17; 17:24-28). God is not only the Creator; God is also the sustainer or maintainer of creation. The story of Noah and the Flood is one illustration among many in the Bible of the sustaining role of God. The thrust of this affirmation is that God is ultimately responsible for creation.

God's responsibility for creation is also expressed in the Christian scriptural tradition through the idea of the Spirit. The story of creation itself begins with the activity of the Spirit in creation. Though God is apart from creation as its creator, God is not distant from creation. God's presence in creation is expressed through scriptural sayings regarding the Holy Spirit. The Psalmist expresses this idea in the most poetic way, when he sings:

> Where can I go from your spirit? Or where can I flee from your presence? If I ascend to heaven, you are there; if I make my bed in Sheol, you are there. If I take the wings of the morning and settle at the farthest limits of the sea, even there your hand shall lead me, and your right hand shall hold me fast. (Ps. 139:7-10)

Moreover, Spirit as immanence is present in creation and is luring it toward growth, flourishing, and fulfillment. One of the most eloquent passages from the writings of Paul (Rom. 8:12-27) illustrates the creative presence of God as Spirit in creation. God, as Creator and Spirit, is the one ultimately responsible for all of creation.

Such a strong affirmation of God as Creator has two distinct effects on the responsibility of humans for each other and for the world around them. First, it redefines responsibility primarily as a response to God and as being responsible to God. As I mentioned earlier, the central affirmation of the Christian faith—namely, that God is the creator of all—makes clear that God's ultimacy means that God is responsible for creation. If God is ultimately responsible, human responsibility can be expressed only as that which is exercised in partnership with God. We can, in our setting, rephrase it this way: God is primarily in mission and we are only God's co-missioners. The primary responsibility of humans is to be responsible to God.

Second, such a view of our responsibility to God relativizes human responsibility. Humans can never claim ultimate responsibility for the earth and those who dwell on it, for only God is *ultimately* responsible. This relativizing power of the concept of God protects human responsibility from its idolatrous and destructive tendencies. The story of the Fall in Genesis 3 is an example of humans arrogating to themselves idolatrous responsibility for themselves and the world around them. The story of Cain, who murders his brother, and the story of the tower of Babel are some ways in which the Hebrew and Christian traditions expose the idolatrous character of human responsibility and call for being responsible to God and exercising our responsibility in partnership with God. One may wonder whether such a heavy emphasis on God's ultimate responsibility for the world would belittle the seriousness with which humans have to exercise their missionary responsibility. It would not. God has created humans in God's image, and the image of God in us invites and enables humans to share in the divine responsibility for the whole of creation (see Gen. 1:26-28). But humans may exercise that responsibility only with a due recognition that theirs is a *relative* responsibility, and hence subordinate to God's *ultimate* responsibility.

To put it differently, humans can exercise their responsibility only in a mode of humility and prayer. Prayer is both the attitude and the mode in which humans act out their missionary responsibility. In discussing the nature of the Christian theological task, Karl Barth writes:

> Dogmatics must always be undertaken as an act of penitence and obedience . . . we merely repeat the statement that dogmatics is possible only as an act of faith, when we point to prayer as the attitude without which there can be no dogmatic work. . . . It must be said, however, that it is hard to see how else there can be successes in this work but on the basis of divine correspondence to this human attitude: "Lord, I believe; help thou mine unbelief."[4]

In a similar vein, we may say that missionary responsibility is an act of prayer in which we willingly accept the relativity of our responsibility and join hands with God in the *missio Dei.*

This relativized understanding of human responsibility and the partnership of God with humans in the carrying out of *missio Dei* is manifested, for the Christian religious tradition, in the life, ministry, crucifixion, and resurrection of Christ. Within the nexus of events surrounding and including Jesus, the cross takes a central place and symbolizes this view of responsibility in two ways. First, missionary responsibility, seen in the light of the cross, can only be expressed as vulnerability. Kosuke Koyama contrasts the "crusading" and "cruciform" modes of missionary enterprise in the past two centuries and argues rightly that cruciform responsibility is specifically a Christian theological understanding.[5] This picture of responsibility emanates from the cross and is exercised through vulnerability and suffering for the sake of others.

In recent times, the centrality of the cross in Christian theological reflection has been severely criticized and boldly questioned by many theologians, especially those who articulate a liberation theology for and with those who are oppressed, exploited, and marginalized in society. For example, Elizabeth Moltman-Wendel lists some of these critiques—those from feminist theologians—and helps us to see how we can rework our theology of the cross.[6] She mentions:

> The cross as it is often preached has often had fatal consequences for women. "Taking up one's cross" could mean patiently tolerating a violent husband, social injustice, and other wrongs that need to remedied. Such preaching of the cross could contribute to keeping women down and

oppressing them. "Crucifying the flesh" has usually been understood as the renunciation of pleasure and joy as crucifying the desires.[7]

Similarly, Roberta Bondi reconstructs a meaningful theology of the cross after reflecting critically and autobiographically on the horrific pictures of the cross Christians have inherited over the years.[8] While we take note of these criticisms, we need to remember that both Moltman-Wendel and Bondi are able to recover the symbol of the cross in much more liberating and emancipatory forms. Moreover, the cross *has*, in fact, functioned as a great liberating force in the history of the modern missionary movement. For example, my own ancestors, who belonged to the lower rungs of the social ladder in India, saw in the cross the vulnerability of God expressed through God's participation in suffering. These were people who lived under the terror and tyranny of local gods and goddesses; they saw the cross as a symbol of God's vulnerability and compassion.

It is interesting to note how theologians in India have viewed the cross as the supreme manifestation of Christ's divinity. For example, K. C. Sen, one of the creative Hindu theologians of nineteenth century India, sees the cross as "a beautiful emblem of self-sacrifice unto the glory of God—one which is calculated to quicken the higher feelings and aspirations of the heart."[9] Similarly, Vengal Chakkarai identifies the cry of dereliction on the cross—"My God, my God, why have you forsaken me?"—as "the precise moment at which the historical Jesus passed over into the Christ."[10] Examining the various ways in which the cross of Christ has informed the people of India, M. M. Thomas says: "In India the crucifixion of Jesus as the symbol of God as Suffering Love identifying himself with the agony of oppressed humanity has been a most potent spiritual vision, inspiring many Indians irrespective of religious or secular labels to identify themselves with the poor and down-troddens."[11]

The way people in different parts of the world have viewed the cross brings into prominence the fact that the cross is also a symbol of protest—a protest against the demonic exercise of human responsibility. Therefore, when I redefine responsibility as cruciform responsibility, I point to both the vulnerability and the protest involved in the cross as Christian symbol.

One further observation is needed before we sum up our idea of cruciform responsibility. The "cruciform" character of our responsibility is informed both by the cross *and* by the resurrection of Jesus the Christ. The resurrection powerfully indicates God's vindication of the vulnerability of the cross and the ultimate protest of God against the injustices of the world that the cross denotes. Therefore the cruciform responsibility of ecclesial communities should take into account the future-oriented responsibility as manifested in the events related to the resurrection of Jesus. When the women came to the tomb on the Easter morning, they were told by the angels: "He [Jesus] has been raised from the dead, and indeed he is going ahead of you to Galilee; there you will see him. This is my message for you" (Matt. 28:7).

Similarly all the resurrection appearances draw the disciples into the future that is "ahead" of them. In discussing the nature of responsibility, one contemporary writer notes that responsibility has "to do with the future. Many ethicists emphasize this. To be responsible means to deliberately, consciously, take responsibility for what is going to happen, for the results of our actions, for the implications of our present behavior, in short, for the future."[12]

The Christian theological understanding of mission needs to be defined as cruciform responsibility. Cruciform responsibility includes a vulnerability that is expressed in situations of suffering and pain, an element of protest and challenge against all demonic forms of responsibility, and an openness to the future ushered in by the risen Christ. The image of God in the human is but the image of the crucified and risen God. This is all the more significant since it is God, and God alone, who is ultimately responsible for the whole of creation and thus relativizes every human responsibility. Cruciform responsibility is that which is exercised in humility and prayer.

Liberative Solidarity

The second element in our portrayal of *missio humanitatis,* "solidarity," takes a significantly unique and interesting direction when placed under the discipline of the Christian view of God in Christ. Let us go back to the picture of the cross that I painted in the earlier section. We find God to be one who exercises God's responsibility in a mode of vulnerability on the cross. It is not a responsibility *for* the other; rather, it is a responsibility *with* the other. This means that God's responsibility is expressed in God's solidarity with the other. The cross is a symbol *par excellence* of God's solidarity. In affirming that Christ suffered for our sake and in our place, the New Testament bears witness to this divine act of solidarity. For example, to remember that Jesus was crucified between two thieves is to perceive God's solidarity with those who are rejected, condemned, and finally killed by humans. The author of the Epistle to the Hebrews expresses the same idea in this manner:

> Since therefore the children share in flesh and blood, he himself likewise partook of the same nature. . . . For surely it is not with angels that he is concerned but with the descendants of Abraham. Therefore he had to be made like his brethren in every respect, so that he might become a merciful and faithful high priest in the service of God. (2:14-17 RSV)

God's concern for humanity and human salvation is expressed through Christ's life of solidarity with the sinful humans.

Coming at this from a feminist theology of the cross, Moltman-Wendel engages the story of the women who were present at the crucifixion to describe the cross as a symbol of solidarity. She finds that most theologians have overlooked this part of the story and goes on to say:

> Two or three women remained under the cross who—unlike the disciples—had not fled. Despite the danger to life and limb, they remained at the place of execution, were present at the death and burial of Jesus, and became the first witnesses to the resurrection. They stayed under the cross out of solidarity and compassion. . . . I regard this tacit counter-theology from the gospels as a theology of the cross. . . .[13]

Thus the cross symbolizes for the Christian disciple the idea of responsibility that is carried out in a mode of solidarity. Writing about the meaning of "Suffering God: Compassion Poured Out," Elizabeth Johnson highlights the idea of solidarity as an extension of the idea of God as love. She writes:

> Love includes willing the good of the beloved, and the classical idea is right as far as it goes. But as actually lived, and paradigmatically so in the light of women's experience, love includes an openness to the ones loved, a vulnerability to their experience, a solidarity with their well-being, so that one rejoices with their joys and grieves with their sorrows. This is not a dispensable aspect of love but belongs to love's very essence.[14]

Johnson also relates solidarity to notions of "compassion" and "responsibility":

> In the midst of the isolation of suffering the presence of divine compassion as companion to the pain transforms suffering, not mitigating its evil but bringing an inexplicable consolation and comfort. . . . Speaking about God's suffering can also help by strengthening human responsibility in the face of suffering. The impassible God models a dispassionate, apathic attitude that influences community ideals. Conversely, the suffering God reorders the human ideal toward compassionate solidarity.[15]

While I highlight the cross as the symbol of responsibility expressed in solidarity, there are ample instances from the life, ministry, and teachings of Jesus that underscore the idea of solidarity as well. To cite one example, the story of Jesus' visit to the home of Zacchaeus as narrated in Luke 19:1-10 illustrates the mode of solidarity with which Jesus practiced his sense of responsibility for and with the other.

The solidarity expressed in the life and ministry of Jesus, the Christ, especially on the cross, has two facets. First, the Christian view of solidarity is incarnational in character. "The Word became flesh and lived among us" (John 1:14) is a central affirmation for Christians. Though God, in and through God's Word, has always been in solidarity with humans, the christological vision of God's solidarity has a "fleshly" character. It is not a solidarity that is expressed through words of compassion from a distance; nor is it a solidarity that is affirmed in purely "spiritual" terms. God's solidarity with humanity is one that is this-worldly, down-to-earth, and concrete. This is what we mean by the incarnational nature of God's solidarity. In whatever ways one may interpret the idea of incarnation,[16] the point of incarnation, as most theologians would agree, is that God's solidarity with humans is expressed in concrete terms. The New Testament and the early church have been vehement about defending the humanity of Jesus precisely because it is this humanity that manifests the "fleshly" solidarity of God with humans. They heavily critiqued and disowned any view of Christ that undermined the humanity of Jesus. For example, John writes: "By this you know the Spirit of God: every spirit that confesses that Jesus Christ has come in the flesh is from God, and every spirit that does not confess Jesus is not from God. And this is the spirit of the antichrist"

(1 John 4:2-3). Thus the solidarity of God with humans is manifested in concrete acts of Jesus' participation in the life of humans.

A Christian theological understanding of mission calls for the expression of solidarity in concrete, "fleshly," and down-to-earth terms. Quite often, Christians have tended to overplay the importance of the *announcement* of the good news of Jesus the Christ and have neglected the *enactment* of the same good news in acts of mercy and justice. Jesus' own parable in Matthew 25:31-46 very aptly illustrates this. One's mission to others is judged on the basis of how one expressed, in concrete terms, solidarity with others.

> I was hungry and you gave me food, I was thirsty and you gave me something to drink, I was a stranger and you welcomed me, I was naked and you gave me clothing, I was sick and you took care of me, I was in prison and you visited me. (vv. 35-36)

The word "compassion" has often been used to denote this incarnational character of solidarity. In feminist writings one comes across the phrase "compassionate solidarity" as a way of expressing the idea of solidarity in concrete acts of being-with-others. For example, Kathleen Talvacchia sees "compassionate solidarity" as "a way to learn to live concretely a passion for justice."[17] Similarly, Wendy Farley, in her phenomenological description of compassion, explains how compassion is not simply a matter of "handwringing sympathy" but rather a "communion with the sufferer in her pain, *as she experiences it.*"[18]

Second, Christian faith defines the nature and purpose of solidarity in very specific terms. In my earlier portrayal of the concept of solidarity, one could detect a certain open-ended-ness. One is invited to express solidarity with *all.* God has expressed, and continues to express, God's solidarity with humans in creating them in God's own image. God is in solidarity with all of humanity, and therefore we are called to be in solidarity with all. While this is true, however, God's solidarity with the whole of humanity is achieved through God's specific and *preferential* solidarity with those who are oppressed, poor, and marginalized. Thus, within the framework of *missio Dei,* and *missio Christi,* solidarity is given a focused meaning.

What does this focused meaning entail? There are at least two aspects. First, the solidarity that is proposed here is clearly a solidarity with those who are poor and marginalized. It is not a solidarity that is devoid of any priorities or preferences. A Christian theological under-standing of solidarity should take seriously into account this "preferen-tial" character of solidarity. As one reads through the pages of the Bible, one is led to see that God expresses God's solidarity preferentially with the poor and the marginalized. The history of the people of Israel, as it unfolds in the Hebrew Bible, is a story of God's preferential solidarity with the slaves in Egypt over against the powerful pharaoh and his armies. In addressing Moses through the miracle of the burning bush, God said: "I have observed the misery of my people who are in Egypt; I have heard their cry on account of their taskmasters. Indeed, I know their sufferings, and I have come down to deliver them from the Egyp-tians" (Exod. 3:7-8). This "preferential option for the poor" (a phrase bequeathed to the global theological community through the writings of the Latin American liberation theologians) winds its way throughout Scripture. David, the youngest and least experienced of his family, is chosen by God to fight the giant Goliath. God is on the side of the three young men who were put into the fiery furnace by Nebuchadnezzar, and on the side of Daniel in the lion's den. Yet this preferential solidarity of God is not limited to the people of Israel alone. While speaking of the liberative acts of God, Amos says that God has been on the side of the suffering and the oppressed in bringing the Philistines from Caphtor and the Syrians from Kir (Amos 9:7).

The same theme is carried over to the life, ministry, death, and res-urrection of Jesus. Jesus begins his ministry at Nazareth by proclaim-ing God's preferential option for the poor. He reads the passage from Isaiah that says

> The Spirit of the Lord is upon me,
> because he has anointed me to bring good news to the poor.
> He has sent me to proclaim release to the captives
> and recovery of sight to the blind,
> to let the oppressed go free,
> to proclaim the year of the Lord's favor.

and goes on to narrate the story of God's priority for the widow of Zarabeth, and for the Syrian general Naaman (Luke 4:16-27). He openly declares, "Blessed are the poor; for theirs is the kingdom of

God," and "I came not to call the righteous but sinners" (see Luke 6:20 and 5:32).

Whenever and wherever this idea of God's "preferential option for the poor" is mentioned, people tend to raise the question: Then what about the rich? The rich, as humans created by God in God's own image, are within the circle of God's solidarity in a general sense. But God's solidarity with the whole of humanity is worked out and achieved in the context of, and in solidarity with, the poor. Ultimately, the reign of God as portrayed in the Gospels is a community where there is neither rich nor poor, neither oppressor nor oppressed; but all are one in the family of God. Therefore, one needs to understand God's preferential solidarity with the poor as a divine activity in between the two great moments in the history of God, namely, God's solidarity with the whole of humanity in creation and God's becoming all in all in the eschaton. Explaining the idea of Jesus' solidarity with the poor in the Gospels, George E. Tinker has this to say:

> From what we can ascertain from the Gospel accounts, Jesus made the explicit choice to walk as the poor among the poor. . . . It is important to note that Jesus was not so much against the people of power or the wealthy as he was in solidarity with the poor.[19]

He continues to argue how this would imply a call to North Americans to "commit themselves to a solidarity with the poor—both of the Southern Hemisphere and with those in our own midst."[20]

Thus the nature of solidarity as articulated from a Christian theological viewpoint is one that sides with the poor and is undergirded by a strong commitment to the poor, the marginalized, and the exploited of our world.

While what I have explained so far pertains to the "nature" of solidarity, the Christian theological viewpoint alters the "purpose" of solidarity as well. What is the goal of this solidarity with the poor? The goal of solidarity—the rich with the poor, and the poor with one another—is for the transformation of the world into a community of justice and peace. Defining "compassionate solidarity" as "a conversion of heart and mind, and a political stance, which intentionally puts oneself in the position of possible suffering in order to effect the just transformation of an injustice against a structurally discriminated group," Talvacchia has this to say:

The just transformation of an injustice against a structurally discriminated group is the goal of compassionate solidarity. This implies that it is an ethical stance which seeks effective action against structural oppression, rather than only denouncing injustice.[21]

Thus, solidarity is not simply for solidarity's sake; it has the express and immediate goal of liberation and justice. So one can say that the Christian theological understanding of mission is not only cruciform responsibility, it is also liberative solidarity—a solidarity that is preferentially expressed with the poor and the marginalized with a view to liberation and justice.

Eschatological Mutuality

The third element in the *missio humanitatis*, mutuality, needs now also to be reconstructed in the light of the Christian theological standpoint. Mutuality is introduced here to further strengthen the idea of solidarity. An overly Christocentric orientation of Christian theology and a narrowly defined understanding of the finality of Christ have tended to keep the idea of mutuality outside the discussion of mission. Mutuality has often been seen as contradictory to the call of mission itself. This is due, I believe, to at least two reasons. First, the biblical and theological views of liberation and justice have often been understood and interpreted in isolation from the idea of mutuality that is strongly present in the biblical and theological traditions. For example, quite often those who quote the "Nazareth Manifesto" in Luke 4 fail to look carefully at the second half of the Lukan pericope. There one discovers that Jesus, while opting for a solidarity for the liberation of the poor, goes on to widen the circle of action to include foreigners such as the widow of Zarabeth and Naaman the Syrian. Therefore, if one carefully examines the biblical and theological traditions, one is led to see that solidarity should be understood in the context of the idea of mutuality.

Second, the idea of the Holy Spirit has been neglected and marginalized due to the "christomonistic" tendencies in much of Christian theology. If one places the ideas of responsibility and solidarity in the context of the doctrine of the Holy Spirit, the idea of mutuality becomes a highly significant addition to a fuller understanding of mission.

In one of his farewell addresses recorded in the Fourth Gospel, Jesus tells his disciples, "I have yet many things to say to you, but you cannot bear them now. When the Spirit of truth comes, he will guide you into all the truth . . . and he will declare to you the things that are to come" (John 16:12-13 RSV). Here the Spirit signifies both the incompleteness of the present and the fullness of the eschaton. When one recognizes this aspect of Christian talk about the Holy Spirit, one is enabled to be open to mutuality. Because the Spirit is significantly related to the eschatological in the New Testament, it is fair to refer to a Christian understanding of mutuality as eschatological mutuality.

Our missionary responsibility demands eschatological mutuality, "for now we see in a mirror dimly, but then face to face. Now I know in part; then I shall understand fully, even as I have been fully understood" (1 Cor. 13:12 RSV). As John writes in one of his letters, "Beloved, we are God's children now; it does not yet appear what we shall be, but we know that when he appears . . . we shall see him as he is" (1 John 3:2 RSV). Therefore, our being-sent-ness involves listening to other religious viewpoints, learning from other religious and secular traditions, and mutually enriching one another toward the eschaton. The kind of eschatological mutuality we are referring to invites us to join the groaning of the whole of creation toward the day of freedom and liberation. As Paul writes, "not only the creation, but we ourselves, who have the first fruits of the Spirit, groan inwardly as we wait for adoption as sons [and daughters], the redemption of our bodies" (Rom. 8:23 RSV).

Furthermore, the experiences of interreligious dialogue and cooperation carried on by various Christian communities throughout the world have also shown how mutuality is necessary for the just transformation of societies into communities of justice and peace. For example, the liberation of the environment from human exploitation requires the spiritual, theological, and human resources of religions other than Christianity. One discovers that the resources available within the Christian tradition are not sufficient for a global involvement in the liberation of the environment. Christians who live as minority groups among people of other religious traditions have always known the significance of mutuality for social transformation. With the emergence of religiously plural communities within largely Christian-dominated societies, those Christians who live in such settings are beginning to recognize the importance of mutuality.

We are now in a position to say that the mission of the church is the working out of its commitment to cruciform responsibility, liberative solidarity, and eschatological mutuality. This is how the Christian community understands *missio humanitatis*. We can safely assume that our dialogue partners are still with us as we outline our idea of *missio humanitatis* from a Christian theological perspective. Once we have offered our reworking of *missio humanitatis*, there are two directions open for us to move forward.

First, we may continue the conversation with our dialogue partners, soliciting their own nuanced understandings of responsibility, solidarity, and mutuality. Once our partners have put forward their views of mission, our dialogue would continue in such a way that we, hopefully, can correct, change, or enhance our own understanding of mission. Furthermore, we may, as a community of conversation, move toward a common understanding of *missio humanitatis*. As far as this book is concerned, we are not in a position to continue this conversation in this way, simply because my dialogue partners (Hindus, Muslims, Jews, and others) are not with me in the writing of the book. Moreover, as I mentioned earlier, the concept of *missio humanitatis* has been used more as a heuristic device or a starting point to help us construct a Christian theology of mission in the context of the widest possible circle of discussion. Our aim was not to arrive at a final version of *missio humanitatis* that all religionists and others would agree upon or feel invested in. Such a project may be of interest to some, but I am not taking that route.

Second, I may choose to move into an intra-Christian conversation and spell out the implications and meanings of the kind of *missio ecclesiae* I have proposed here. This is the route I am taking at this point in time. I will use my exposition of the mission of humanity (cruciform responsibility, liberative solidarity, and eschatological mutuality) as the working theology of mission and expound the implications of this understanding for the various aspects of mission, such as evangelism, social action, church growth, and so on. Then I will move to reread both the biblical materials and the history of Christianity from the perspective of the theology of mission worked out so far. Finally, we will also examine how one might go about motivating our Christian congregations to engage in such a mission.

4

Issues in Mission

We began our inquiry into a relevant theology of mission for today by outlining the new situation in which we find ourselves. I mapped out the two overriding elements: a widening of the circle of discussion and a crisis of confidence. Taking note of this situation meant that we needed to find a new starting point for constructing a theology of mission. I suggested that a discussion of the mission of humanity *(missio humanitatis)* would assist us in this process. Therefore, I expounded the mission of humanity in terms of *responsibility, solidarity,* and *mutuality.* Then we proceeded to flesh out a Christian theology of mission, taking into account both *missio Dei* and *missio Christi.* That led us to define the mission of the church in the broadest possible manner as *cruciform responsibility, liberative solidarity,* and *eschatological mutuality.* Thus the mission of the church is to live out its commitment to the three realities mentioned above. In other words, the church is invited to act with a sense of responsibility that is informed by the vision of the Crucified God; in a mode of solidarity that, in its preference to the poor, works toward the liberation of the whole of humanity; and permeated by a spirit of mutuality that, being led by the Holy Spirit, engages with a vision of the eschaton of love, justice, and peace.

One may wonder whether we have, in fact, lost sight of some of the traditional yet significantly important issues related to the mission of the church by the route we took in formulating a theology of mission and by the conclusions we reached with regard to the mission of the church. Issues such as evangelism, conversion, church growth, social service, verbal proclamation of the good news in Jesus the Christ, and so forth have all been lost on the way, one may think. I would argue, however, that such is not necessarily the case, although certainly each of these issues needs to be redefined and reformulated within the new perspective developed herein. In particular, our understanding of these elements of mission must be shaped by a spirit of dialogue and mutuality. It is to this task that I turn in this chapter. I shall examine each of these issues with the goal of reinterpreting and restating them within the broad theology of mission I have here proposed.

1. Mission and Evangelism

Evangelism is an issue that has been greatly debated in the life of the churches in the twentieth century. This is evident in the variety of definitions of "evangelism" one may come across. These vary from "Evangelism is social action,"[1] to evangelism as "announcing the gospel to non-Christians with a view to faith and conversion and their eventual incorporation into the Church by baptism."[2] One can detect a broad spectrum of definitions. While some emphasize the task of proclamation, others highlight the acting out of the gospel in and through acts of mercy. Some try to combine the various elements that are highlighted in these differing definitions into either a single definition or a set of guidelines. For example, George Morris defines evangelism as "spreading the gospel of the kingdom of God by word and deed and then waiting in respectful humility and working with expectant hope."[3] David Bosch lists a set of eighteen propositions to get to a constructive understanding of evangelism today. These propositions include "I perceive mission to be wider than evangelism," "Evangelism is always an invitation," and "Evangelism is not the same as church extension."[4] Thus we are dealing here with an area where one finds a variety of opinions and a host of ambiguities. Therefore, let me begin by highlighting the history of the term "evangelism" and then examining the implications of our theology of mission for an understanding of evangelism.

Christian theologians today employ both the term "evangelism" and the term "evangelization." While for most readers these two are synonymous, broadly speaking one may say that "evangelization" is most often used by Roman Catholics and some Evangelicals, whereas the term "evangelism" is more prevalent among ecumenically minded Protestant Christians. These two groups may mean different things by these two terms. Nevertheless, it is clear that these terms are late arrivals in the history of mission. As Kenneth Cracknell notes:

> The terms "evangelism" and "evangelization" are comparative late-comers in Christian vocabulary. Rare indeed are the sightings of either term before the mid-nineteenth century. An evangelist was one of the writers of the four Gospels or a title of an office in the early church, and that virtually was it![5]

Therefore, it is wise to look at the roots of the word "evangelism." This word comes from the Greek words *euangelion* (good news) and *euangelizomai* (to preach the good news), as they come to us from the New Testament. Jesus begins his ministry by announcing, "The time is fulfilled, and the kingdom of God has come near; repent, and believe in the good news."[6] The Greek term *euangelion* is made up of two words: *eu* (good) and *angelion* (message). The term "evangelism," therefore, can be defined as the act of preaching or proclaiming the good news of Jesus the Christ.

One needs to note that in the New Testament use of these terms, two major ideas emerge. First, the good news is most often the good news of the "kingdom" of God, though in a few places the good news is associated with Christ or simply God. It is good news about the coming or the already-come reign of God. Second, the verb form *(euangelizomai)* need not necessarily be translated as *preaching* the good news. One may literally translate it as "good-news-ing." In other words, *euangelizomai* could very well be translated as "living the good news" or "being the good news."

While we note the New Testament usage of these terms, we need to bear in mind that the words "mission" and "evangelism" have come to have varied meanings—sometimes as similar to one another, and other times as distinct from one another—in the history of the church, especially in this century. When the leaders of the Edinburgh conference in

1910 brought their earlier slogan, "the evangelization of the world in our generation," they were not too particular or specific about the difference between the terms "mission" and "evangelism." But since then, these two terms have come to a process of change in their meanings. When the ecumenical movement progressed under the Life and Work Movement and the Faith and Order Movement, it seemed that the peculiar thrust of Christian mission for the proclamation of the Christian message was being lost in the ecumenical discussion. While the Faith and Order Movement was concerned with seeking unity at the level of doctrine, the Life and Work Movement focused on unity that is brought about through participation in acts, programs, and events of service to the community at local and global levels. These two movements appeared to have lost sight of the proclamatory character of mission. As a response to this, the International Missionary Council was formed in 1921. Though the IMC emphasized the role of "evangelism" in the life of the churches, it was more concerned about unity in mission. The terms "mission" and "evangelism" had not yet been set over against each other. Between 1921 and 1961, the rise of the evangelical movement in the United States and Europe had begun to distinguish sharply the understanding of "mission" from that of "evangelism." The result was that when the IMC finally joined the WCC to form the Commission on World Mission and Evangelism, the two words had to be coupled together in the naming of this commission; neither could stand by itself.

These two words came to be used in three sets of meanings. First, while mission meant the outreach activity of the church in service, evangelism was seen as the proclaiming of the Lordship of Christ and inviting people to join the church. In other words, while mission emphasized the *activities* of love, justice, and peace, evangelism highlighted the verbal *announcing* of the good news of Jesus Christ. One could engage in mission without mentioning the name of Christ; but it is not so with evangelism, where one is called upon to name the name of Christ and invite people to accept Christ as their Savior and Lord. Second, while mission came more and more to be associated with "overseas" missionary efforts, evangelism came to mark the efforts of the local church to preach the gospel to its immediate neighbors and invite them to join the church. While "mission" came to conjure up images of the hungry, poor, and destitute in the so-called third world, "evangelism" stood for what one might call a membership drive in local churches. This distinction is clearly seen in churches in the U.S.A. that have two separate committees or boards, one for mission (overseas) and one for evangelism (local membership drive). Third, some defined "mission" as a broader term that included both acts of charity and the ministry of announcing the good news. This meant that the word "evangelism" was more and more limited to the verbal proclamation of the good news of Jesus Christ.

Such a sharp distinction between "mission" and "evangelism" was further strengthened by the Lausanne Committee on World Evangelization which called evangelicals all over the world to be united under the banner of "evangelization." The word "evangelization" came to be seen as more inclusive than the word "mission."[7] This was, in part, a reaction against the marginalization of the word "evangelism" to simply mean the verbal proclamation within ecumenical circles. It was also a way of regaining the word "evangelization" in its fuller meaning, that is, as both announcing and living the good news.

Today we are in a situation of chaos and ambiguity with regard to the use of these two terms. This is very clear in the way in which David Bosch proposes eighteen guidelines for the understanding of evangelism. He goes through highly dialectical propositions to get to a nuanced understanding. For example, he says, "Evangelism is not the same as church extension," and immediately follows that by saying, "To distinguish between evangelism and membership recruitment is not to suggest, though, that they are disconnected."[8]

Given this ambiguity of the definition of the word "evangelism," let me propose a working definition of the term "evangelism" that will allow us to see how evangelism can function within the overall theological scheme I have outlined. According to this working definition, evangelism is the task of sharing the good news of Jesus the Christ and inviting people to a personal commitment to Christ and consequently to join the church.

The theology of mission we have worked out maintains that Christians who have been formed and transformed by the good news of Jesus the Christ have the responsibility of sharing that good news with their neighbors. We mentioned that mission is an act of responsibility. To be responsible is to share. If one thinks that the story of Jesus is something precious and transformative, one would simply be exercising one's sense of responsibility by retelling that story to his or her neighbors. Therefore, evangelism is a rightful and legitimate activity of the local church. But it has to be a *cruciform* activity. The sharing of the good news ought to be done in a spirit of vulnerability and humility. Remember that the Christian act of responsibility has to be chastened by the vision of the cross as God's expression of the divine responsibility through vulnerability and suffering. Those who reject evangelism as unnecessary and even "unchristian" fail to see that evangelism done in a cruciform spirit is not conquest-minded or militant. Writing on the vulnerability of mission, David Bosch draws from writings of Ronald Allen and D. T. Niles and goes on to say:

> Allen, who was comparing Paul's missionary methods with ours, was actually suggesting the model of the "victim" missionary. So was D. T. Niles, one of the most remarkable Third World Christians of our time, who was wont to depict mission or evangelism as one beggar telling other beggars where to find bread. The point is that we are as dependent on the bread as those are to whom we go. And it is only as we share it with them that we experience its true taste and nutritious value.[9]

When evangelism is marked by this sense of cruciform responsibility, the question of church growth takes on a different tone and color. Our invitation to others to join the church is done in vulnerability, and therefore it cannot be seen simply as a membership *drive*. It will always remain as an invitation, and that makes church growth a possible by-product of evangelism and not the norm or measuring rod for the effectiveness of evangelism. This is clearly expressed in the way the evangelistic task of the church is portrayed in the book of the Acts of the Apostles. For example, the disciples share the good news of Jesus Christ in ordinary, unplanned, and spontaneous situations; and they continue to maintain that it was God who was bringing people into the fellowship of the church. Every preaching situation of the early disciples is marked by its unexpected and unplanned character. Acts 2:46-47 reads: "Day by day, as they spent much time together in the temple . . . praising God and having the goodwill of all the people. And day by day the Lord added to their number those who were being saved." One can argue that Donald McGavran's way of highlighting church growth as the sign of faithfulness to the task of evangelization is misleading and biblically unsound. When he defines "today's supreme task" as "effective multiplication of churches in the receptive societies of earth,"[10] and when he says, "today's paramount task, opportunity, and imperative in missions is to multiply churches,"[11] we need to note that such a view of church growth makes it a goal and measuring rod of evangelism rather than a by-product.

In the history of the missionary movement, one can clearly see that not all those who heard the good news of Jesus the Christ felt the need to join the church. There have always been individuals and groups of people who accepted the Lordship of Christ in their lives, lived a life of discipleship, and never joined the fellowship of the church. Mahatma Gandhi, who followed the teachings of Jesus with a great sense of commitment and determination, never saw the need for joining the church. There is a group of Christians in the town of Sivakasi in South India who have been known as "secret Christians" for decades. These are rich women in the business community who secretly admire and follow Christ. But they have refrained from accepting baptism and publicly joining the local church for personal and family reasons. The local congregation has itself been very supportive of their decision to remain "secret." One further illustration of this is the life and work of Simone Weil. In describing her life, Diogenes Allen has this to say: "Weil is . . . an outsider to institutional Christianity. . . . She was critical of superficial understanding of Christianity which can be found both inside and outside the Church. . . . She was born a Jew and was never baptized."[12] While she was never baptized, Weil did claim herself to be a Christian and believed in many of the central doctrines of the Christian faith. She was more upset by the exclusive claims of Christianity than by any other beliefs. Thus one can maintain that effective "evangelism" is neither always nor necessarily followed by church growth in the institutional sense.

When we apply the idea of "liberative solidarity" to the task of evangelism, we notice some significant implications. First of all, it is crystal clear that the kind of "hit-and-run-evangelism" that is practiced in several churches is due severe criticism. Let me illustrate what I mean here with the following autobiographical notes. As an evangelistically minded layperson, and later as a minister in the Church of South India, I have participated in the evangelistic programs of my church. Quite often, local congregations will choose a village or town several miles away from them to engage in evangelistic work. A team of Christians will go to that village, preach on the various street corners, distribute a few tracts and booklets, and return home in a few hours. In such a case there is practically no expression at all of being "with" those who are the objects of one's evangelistic efforts. These are occasional and sporadic visits that do not generally lead to a fostering of friendships and relationships. I have a photograph from one of these evangelistic visits that shows me handing over a tract to a person in a village far from my home town. I am a nineteen-year-old college graduate dressed in long dark pants, white shirt, and flashy tie; and I am giving this tract to an older gentleman who is much less formally educated, wearing the South Indian *dhoti*, and naked above the waist. The moment I gave him the tract was the only moment that I had any contact with that gentleman at all. I handed it to him and left the spot immediately, hence the term "hit-and-run" evangelism. The theology of mission that I propose looks upon such sporadic acts of evangelism as lacking any expression of solidarity. Such evangelism fails to recognize and practice the incarnational dimension of the Christian faith.

Another issue surfaces here as well. I earlier defined mission as *liberative* solidarity. In mission we express our solidarity with the poor and work with them towards their, and eventually everyone's, liberation. Let me take you back to that photograph, where I look very much like a middle-class, educated, and economically privileged person in comparison to the older gentleman, who is a poor, landless laborer. While I was giving the tract to him, I was totally unaware of the kind of economic and social conditions in which he lived. Nor was I mindful of the fact that the good news that I shared with him had serious implications for his liberation from the oppressive conditions under which he lived. Here was an evangelistic task that failed to express solidarity and neglected the liberative power of the gospel.

Evangelism that is limited to verbal proclamation of the good news is to be questioned on both biblical and contextual grounds. Biblically, as we noted earlier, evangelism includes sharing the good news in word *and* deed. It is about the establishment of the Reign of God, which is a community of justice and peace.

The third element in the theology of mission I have outlined is *eschatological mutuality*. Christian mission should take seriously the mutuality that comes from its openness to the movement of the Spirit in the world. We are called upon to listen to one another, to learn, correct, and challenge one another in our missionary enterprise. This means, then, that evangelism cannot be a one-way street. While we bear witness to the love of God manifested in the life, death, and resurrection of Jesus the Christ, our neighbors of other religious traditions and ideologies should be allowed to share their witness with us. Only then will evangelism be an exercise in mutuality.

One may say that the Christian church has always listened to those outside of its membership. Did not the missionaries listen to the native peoples in the various countries? How could they have translated the Bible into the languages of the various peoples if they had not listened to them? Christians have often listened to people of other traditions, most often to supply us with their questions to which we may present Christ as the answer. The kind of mutual witnessing I would propose, however, is that which allows the partners to listen and witness to one another. While a Christian shares the good news of Jesus Christ, a Hindu may share with the Christian the way he or she had come to witness God's dealing with him or her in their faith-community. Such a willingness to allow the other to witness to us is founded on a vision of the eschaton in which all are brought into a community of peace, justice, and love.

On the basis of what I have said so far, we begin to see that evangelism in light of the proposed theology of mission can only be done in a mode of vulnerability and humility, can only be aimed at the holistic liberation of peoples, and can only be exercised in a setting of mutual witness. Such a form of evangelism may or may not lead to people joining the church.

This discussion of evangelism has, I think, shown how we are called upon to redefine evangelism in dialogical terms and in a spirit of mutuality. It is interesting to note that Kenneth Cracknell ends his book on evangelism with these words:

> For most people the good news has to be told for the first time. Perhaps they are people who live within one of the great world religions. . . . For all such people that Christian message needs to be made known in a way in which they can understand it, question it, bring their own insights to bear upon it, and make their own response to it. This requires "discernment, seriousness, respect and competence." The way in which this will happen is more likely to be dialogue than proclamation. And the process itself, by the grace of God, will lead us to a place where neither they nor we have ever been before.[13]

Thus any discussion of evangelism in light of our theology of mission will invariably lead us to examine the idea of dialogue, which I take up later in this chapter.

2. Mission and Conversion

Our discussion of evangelism has not yet highlighted the idea of religious conversion. But the ideas of church growth and membership recruitment have close connections to the idea of conversion. Therefore it is logical and necessary that we discuss the idea of conversion in this section. The history of the missionary movement in the last three centuries and the perception of Christian mission by those outside the Christian tradition have turned the word "conversion" into a dirty word. Many Christians themselves appropriate that view of conversion and feel guilty about their past missionary involvement, and would heartily recommend that people be left alone in the religious traditions that they are born with. Mahatma Gandhi was vehemently opposed to this Christian view of conversion. Gandhi categorically said once: "I am against conversion, whether it is known as *shuddhi* by Hindus, *tabligh* by Mussalmans or proselytizing by Christians."[14] Such criticisms of "conversion" have altered the view of Christian mission in such a way that mission or evangelism is equated with "change of religion" at its best sense and "proselytism" in its most pejorative sense. A careful examination of these issues is in order if one is to make theological judgments on the nature and purpose of conversion.

My first real encounter with the word as such was in 1961, when I read for the first time a book on conversion by the famous Methodist missionary in India, E. Stanley Jones.[15] His book had a profound influence on me at that time and continues to inspire me today. Though I had encountered the English word "conversion" in Jones's book, the experience of conversion was very real to me both in the history of my Christian ancestors and in my own history.

Stanley Jones quotes William James's definition of conversion. It goes like this:

> To be converted, to be regenerated, to receive grace, to experience religion, to gain assurance, are so many phrases which denote the process, gradual or sudden, by which a self, hitherto divided, and consciously wrong, inferior and unhappy, becomes unified and consciously right,

superior and happy, in consequence of its firmer hold upon religious realities.[16]

While Stanley Jones appreciates this definition as "sound and penetrating in its psychological phases," he finds it theologically insufficient because it does not refer to the commitment to a Person (like the person of Jesus the Christ) in the process of conversion. Taking James's definition of conversion as it is, one can see that conversion is a very positive experience, and one would wish all the more that one would have such experiences.

Our theology of mission, if exercised in the way in which it has been outlined in this chapter (both in evangelism and dialogue), should lead one to expect a regeneration, a reception of grace by all peoples of the world. In this sense, conversion is strongly recommended for all. Evangelism and dialogue do lead to conversion. People who announce the good news and the people who hear it do experience a conversion. They come to a "firmer hold upon religious realities." Such conversion can take different forms. It may take the form of one's revision and reformulation of one's own religious tradition. For example, some of the Hindu reformers in India, such as Raja Ram Mohan Roy, Keshub Chunder Sen, Vivekananda, Mahatma Gandhi, and Radhakrishnan, were converted to a new form of Hindu faith and practice. In some cases, it may lead to leaving one's native tradition, community, and beliefs behind and joining a totally new community and tradition. My own ancestors chose this kind of a conversion. They moved from popular Hinduism and its traditions to an Anglican form of Christianity. Some others were converted to taking Jesus' teachings and his self-sacrifice on the cross as their leading religious symbols while continuing to be a Hindu or a secularist. As M. M. Thomas puts it, "in India the crucifixion of Jesus as the symbol of God as Suffering Love identifying himself with the agony of the oppressed humanity has been a most potent spiritual vision, inspiring many Indians irrespective of religious or secular labels to identify themselves with the poor and the down-troddens."[17] In all these cases, one thing is clear: people experienced conversion.

Similarly, in the case of dialogue one can venture to say that no dialogue ends without some form of conversion—a conversion to a "firmer hold upon religious realities." I have come away from such dialogues with a great sense of discovering something that I had not known for years in my own religious tradition. Or I may find the strangeness and novelty of the other's religious tradition so challenging that I find myself converted to a new way of looking at the reality around me. It is also possible that in and through dialogue one may come to discover the insufficiency of one's own tradition for meeting one's spiritual needs and may decide to move to another religious tradition. Conversion is a real possibility in interreligious dialogue as well.

Our view of mission as responsibility, solidarity, and mutuality gives us a wide variety of possibilities in conversion. Conversion is not limited to a change of religion alone. Conversion is a two-way street, and it can go in all directions. But the question that needs to be addressed is this: To what should people be converted? Let us turn our attention to this very question.

3. Mission and Transformation

It is becoming clear to us that the task of Christian mission is not simply either to proclaim verbally the good news in Jesus the Christ or to recruit more members for the Christian church all over the globe. If that is the case, what exactly is the purpose of Christian mission? Does not our mission aim for some change in the hearers or recipients and the world in which this mission is taking place? How shall we describe and articulate that purpose in meaningful and concrete terms within the framework of our theological proposal?

Let me begin by proposing a more generic term for what mission desires to accomplish. Mission is for *transformation*. It is interesting to note that David Bosch titles his monumental volume on mission "Transforming Mission" and begins the book with a discussion of the ambiguity in the title. While his book, as he claims, is a descriptive account of the dramatic transformations or changes that have happened in the church's understanding and practice of her mission, he maintains that mission is "an enterprise that transforms reality."[18] He goes on to write that mission, according to his perspective, is "that dimension of our faith that refuses to accept reality as it is and aims at changing it. 'Transforming' is, therefore, an adjective that depicts an essential feature of what Christian mission is all about."[19] But the word "transformation" is a formal one. It does not have any material content to it. What kind of transformation are we talking about with regard to mission? What does the present reality look like and what would a transformed reality look like? I address these questions under three dimensions.

a. The transformation that is aimed at by mission is a *personal* transformation. This dimension of transformation is signified by several terms, such as "salvation," "conversion," "regeneration," "being born again," and so on. It is one of the major elements in the transformation that is aimed at by Christian mission. This is built on the theological premise that humans are lost, sinful, and uncentered in their personal and individual lives. Stanley Jones calls such a transformation a "conversion from a self-centered person to a God-centered person."[20] Some others may use phrases such as "accepting the Lord Jesus Christ as one's personal Lord and Savior." What is articulated here is the missional task of helping people transform themselves into centered and holistic humans. The gospel of Jesus the Christ offers a way and a power to transform one's stunted and disoriented life into a flourishing one through faith, hope, and love. Paul invites his readers, "Do not be conformed to this world, but be *transformed* by the renewing of your minds, so that you may discern what is the will of God—what is good and acceptable and perfect."[21] The history of missions, from the New Testament times to the present, is filled with examples of those who found such a personal transformation through the Christian gospel.

The theological framework that I have offered so far (cruciform responsibility, etc.) does support and promote such a link between mission and transformation on a personal level. Taking responsibility for others in the spirit of the cross does involve offering the personal transformation available in the Christian gospel to those around us. It is not offered because we who offer are fully transformed and perfect. But in humility and hope Christ is offered as one who transforms people on an individual and personal level. There are three considerations that our theology of mission invites us to bear in mind when it comes to this idea of personal transformation. First, the processive understanding of evangelism and mission that we have put forward would not insist on personal transformation as a one-time, dramatic event. Personal transformation is a long and lifetime journey of change and growth. It cannot be limited to, though in some cases it may include, an "on-the-road-to-Damascus" sort of experience. Second, the other elements in the idea of transformation, such as the societal and ecological aspects, should also be given serious consideration. Mission cannot be limited to individual and personal transformation alone. Christian mission is not simply concerned with the psychological dimension of one's life. The gospel is addressed to the whole human being. Third, if our mission is done in a spirit of solidarity and mutuality, then the personal transformative elements in traditions other than our own will have to be acknowledged and celebrated. For example, if my Muslim or Hindu friend shares with me his or her experience of personal transformation through his or her tradition, I need to recognize this as a valid and true experience of transformation and see such instances as enhancing my own journey toward being a fully centered human.

b. The transformation to which mission aims is a societal transformation. The word "societal" is used here to mean the social, political, and economic dimensions of human life. The history of missions shows how the church has always been concerned not simply about individuals but with societies, nations, and the globe itself. The dramatic social changes brought about by Christian mission throughout the world bear witness to this. The establishment of schools, colleges, hospitals, and similar institutions due to Christian missionary work has brought more social changes to those peoples than the churches themselves that were planted on those soils. Moreover, the Christian gospel, from its very beginning, has been a gospel of intense political and economic change. For example, when the early Christians proclaimed Jesus as Lord, they were making a political statement of protest against the lordship of the Caesars, whether they were conscious of it or not. The existence of the *ecclesia* as a countercultural community in the midst of a larger society (for example, in the common sharing of bread, property, and goods with each other as recorded in the first few chapters of Acts) was itself an invitation to societal transformation. The very missionary enterprise that saw the expansionist policies of the British Empire in India as a blessing in disguise for the spread of the gospel offered an incentive and motivation for the dramatic political changes that happened in India through the Independence Movement, under the leadership of Mahatma Gandhi and others. Furthermore, most often conversion to Christianity was a strong and powerful protest against the status quo of sociopolitical and economic reality, and aimed at transforming that reality with a vision of the reign of God as preached and lived out by Jesus in the Gospels. Thus, mission aims at broad societal transformation.

Our theological framework promotes such a societal transformation. The idea of responsibility and solidarity we have put forward really aims at such drastic political and economic changes. The idea of cruciform responsibility does not see the cross simply as a symbol of self-sacrifice; rather, it highlights the cross as a powerful protest against the political and economic powers of Jesus' day. Yet I would like to add three considerations in understanding mission as societal transformation. First, we need to be self-conscious about the political character of mission and the political implications of mission. A lack of awareness of the "political" side allows an idea of mission to fall prey to the dominant political ideology of the given moment, and thus does not ultimately contribute to societal transformation; rather, it only strengthens the status quo and by its silence fails to transform reality. For example, when an elementary school is established in a small, remote village in any part of the world, one is engaging in highly explosive political and economic activity (although the true character of that activity may take a while to come to fruition). One needs to be aware of this. Such awareness will formulate and direct the particular educational program in ways that one had not thought of before. Second, the kind of "liberative" solidarity that we have put forward demands that one pay attention to the sociopolitical and economic structures of society. It is not enough to organize instruments of charity (charity understood as almsgiving); rather, one should set in motion a movement that attempts to alter the prevailing unjust structures of a society that perpetuates poverty, inequality, and oppression. Thanks to Latin American Liberation theologians, we have been conscientized with regard to the primacy of structures in dealing with societal problems. Thus, legal, organizational, and constitutional changes are all very much a part of the program of mission that aims at societal transformation. Third, our idea of "eschatological mutuality" demands that our engagement in societal transformation cannot and should not be achieved in isolation from other communities of faith and commitment. Our partners in other religious and secular traditions are our companions in our journey toward a just and peaceful community all over the world. To use the words of George Rupp, we are called to establish "communities of collaboration" that celebrate our "shared commitments and common tasks."[22]

c. The transformation that is aimed at by mission is *ecological* transformation. We live in a time of heightened awareness about the ecological problems of the world. Several international conferences and congresses have met during the last two decades to increase this awareness. The Earth Summit at Rio de Janeiro especially has "elevated the awareness of people and their leaders to the crisis our civilization faces as a result of the damage we are inflicting on our earth's environment and development goals. Rio altered the environment and development dialogue fundamentally, linking poverty, equity and social justice with the achievement of sustainable development."[23] Thus, today we are keenly aware that the personal and societal dimensions of human life are closely interwoven with the ecological dimension. Therefore, mission should promote and work for ecological transformation.

The ideas of responsibility, solidarity, and mutuality that we have examined give a strong foundation and impetus for engaging in healthy and sustainable ecological transformation. They also warn us against an irresponsible and excessive exploitation of nature and the environment to satisfy the greed of humans and their societies. As I had mentioned earlier in the discussion of *missio ecclesiae*, we need to express our responsibility with a deep sense of solidarity and mutuality with all living beings and nonliving things in the universe. The idea of "Emmanuel" in the Gospels calls us to proclaim and live out the continuing presence of God in creation. I have referred to this elsewhere as the "emmanuelization of creation."[24] Our ecological mission is the emmanuelization of the whole creation. One can see how the personal and the societal dimensions of transformation come together in the task of ecological transformation. As Constantin Voicu writes, "A better environment will never exist without a more just social order."[25] Similarly, a better environment will not be available to humans if there is not a personal transformation in humans that leads to a loving and sharing attitude toward the earth and a lifestyle that promotes simplicity and love.

To sum up, both evangelism and conversion necessarily involve transformation. While not exhaustive, the above remarks indicate personal, societal, and ecological dimensions of the transformation that the theology of mission proposed here involve.

4. Mission and Dialogue

One other issue needs our careful attention, namely, the idea of dialogue or conversation. We have used dialogue as a significant and guiding element in the articulation and practice of our theological method-ology. At this point, we need to note that dialogue is not simply a methodology; it is a way of being in mission as well.

Dialogue, as a form of missionary obedience, has been an important part of the life of the church right from its beginning. Paul, the greatest missionary of his time, saw dialogue as a form of witness in his missionary journeys. One can see, in the Acts of the Apostles, how Paul practiced the discipline of dialogue in his ministry. Commenting on Paul's missionary journeys, Wesley Ariarajah says: "Even though Paul's ministry led to discussion and controversy within his community, we cannot assume that he was an unsympathetic or uncompromising preacher who gave his message on a 'take it or leave it' basis. In many places he spent a good deal of time in dialogue."[26] Ariarajah goes on to show how Paul is said to have had several discussions in Ephesus where he lived for two years and how the Greek word that is used to describe these discussions is "dialogue." Thus all along the history of the early church and through our history, dialogue has been a significant part of missionary obedience. A high view of dialogue that considers it as a form of witness was lost during the missionary era of the last three centuries, and in its place dialogue came to be seen purely in instrumental terms. Dialogue was seen as a preparation for witness and not witness itself. This was perhaps due to the ethos that surrounded the missionary movement, which arose from the colonial expansion of the West and the assumed superiority of Western civilization.

Dialogue has increasingly become a form of witness during the last decades, especially through the work of the World Council of Churches and the writings of theologians from Asia and Africa. When Stanley Samartha, a leading Christian theologian from India, was asked to head the Subunit of the WCC on Dialogue with Living Faiths and Ideologies in 1971, dialogue (specifically interreligious dialogue) had become a household term in the ecumenical ecclesial communities. This subunit organized several formal dialogues with people of other religions and ideologies, and various conferences were held from then on. One of the significant milestones in the life of this subunit was the production of a set of guidelines called *Guidelines on Dialogue with People of Living Faiths and Ideologies* in 1979.[27] Churches all over the world were invited to study this document and engage in dialogue in their own local settings. Such an invitation did not go without a response. Many churches, seminaries, and other ecclesial groups have been engaged in this type of dialogue over the years.

The history of the discussion on dialogue within the Protestant ecumenical circles has gone through three different stages. The first stage was to look for a theology *for* dialogue—a theology that would justify engaging in dialogue as witness rather than a strategy for conversion of the other. One was called to defend dialogue as a biblically and theologically legitimate ecclesial and missionary practice. Ariarajah's book *The Bible and the People of Other Faiths* belongs to this stage. The second stage was a search for a theology *of* dialogue in which dialogue was looked at as a theological concern. One needed to discuss the relation between dialogue and evangelism, dialogue and social action, and other such relationships. Here one would come across discussion of the types of dialogue and their theological meanings. The third stage is one in which one attempts to address questions such as: What is the theological view of religious plurality as such? What does it mean to do theology in the context of such ongoing dialogues between Christians and people of other religions? What are the implications of interreligious dialogue for theological method and theological content? One can detect two directions with regard to this. On the one hand, one is compelled more and more to work out a theology of religions that takes note of the religious pluralism of today and the apparent parity between religious traditions. Several theologians have been engaged in this task in recent years. John Hick, Paul Knitter, Mark Heim, Clark Pinnock, John Sanders, and others have been involved in this, to name a few. The WCC itself has been engaged in this task of working out a theology of religions in its conferences over the last few years. On the other hand, one is invited to construct one's Christian theology in dialogue with other traditions. My own work in *The Crucified Guru* was one such construction.[28] Another example is the most recent book by Francis Clooney, titled *Seeing Through Texts: Doing Theology Among the Srivaisnavas of South India.*[29] The question here is: What would it mean to construct a Christian theology in light of the experiences of and the learnings from interreligious dialogue?

As far as the Roman Catholics are concerned, Vatican II gave a boost to the engagement in and the promotion of interreligious dialogue. Pope Paul VI established a separate Secretariat for Non-Christians. At present this Secretariat is called the Pontifical Council for Interreligious Dialogue. Since then several encyclicals and documents have been published by the Vatican encouraging the Roman Catholics to engage in dialogue as a form of witness. The document "Dialogue and Proclamation" published by the Council in 1991 is a milestone in the life of the Roman Catholic Church. Currently the Pontifical Council for Interreligious Dialogue and the Office of Interreligious Relations of the World Council of Churches hold consultations together and thus promote the ministry of dialogue. As Jose Kuttianimattathil writes:

> In the period subsequent to the Second Vatican Council both the practice and theology of interreligious dialogue have advanced considerably. Dialogue owes this progress to the pioneers who ventured into unknown territory and refused to give up in the face of opposition; the myriads of ordinary people living a daily life of dialogue by recognizing and accepting the other as different; . . . the perseverance and hope of the many men and women who met and still meet to share and to pray.[30]

Though evangelical theologians have been suspicious and skeptical of dialogue as a form of witness in the earlier decades of this half of the century, today more and more of them begin to affirm the need for dialogue to be recognized as a form of witness and mission. Of course, the Lausanne Covenant, the historic document of evangelicals on world evangelization, mentions dialogue only in passing and only in reference to understanding the hearer of the word.[31] This is not a common understanding among all evangelical theologians, and yet there is an increasing number of them who see dialogue as genuine form of witness.

Before we examine how dialogue functions within the theology of mission that we have mapped out, let me mention a few more details about what dialogue is all about. Dialogue is best understood when one looks at the types and goals of dialogue. The Roman Catholic document "Dialogue and Proclamation" lists four types of dialogue.

(a) The *dialogue of life,* where people strive to live in an open and neighborly spirit, sharing their joys and sorrows, their human problems and preoccupations.
(b) The *dialogue of action,* in which Christians and others collaborate for the integral development and liberation of people.
(c) The *dialogue of theological exchange,* where specialists seek to deepen their understanding of their respective religious heritages, and to appreciate each other's spiritual values.

(d) The *dialogue of religious experience,* where persons, rooted in their own religious traditions, share their spiritual riches, for instance with regard to prayer and contemplation, faith and ways of searching for God or the Absolute.[32]

I find this a very helpful classification of the types of dialogue. One can easily see that each of these types is governed by a set of goals. The dialogue of life is aimed at promoting harmonious living in communities of pluralistic religious persuasion. The sharing in the "joys and sorrows" and in the "problems and preoccupations" is very much in line with the kind of cruciform responsibility that I have referred to in the previous chapter. This is done in the most spontaneous but intentional way of living among people of other traditions and beliefs. In such a dialogue one also detects an experience of solidarity and mutuality. Sharing the joys and sorrows of others is nothing but a concrete form of practicing solidarity. Such a sharing is always mutual and thus promotes the kind of eschatological mutuality we have talked about earlier.

The dialogue of action aims at addressing the problems of the human community (at the local, regional, and national levels) and redressing the injustices that are rampant in our communities. This form of dialogue is all the more concrete and incarnational. It is something in which we take responsibility for our earth together with other people. Such a posture saves us from "crusading" responsibility and places us squarely in a mode of "cruciform" responsibility. We place ourselves as partners in the march toward a liberated community of justice and peace. Such dialogues of action are supreme examples of our engaging in liberative solidarity. We are one with others in "the integral development and liberation of people." Such engagement invariably calls for a spirit of mutuality—of give and take—in all our activities and programs. For example, Habitat for Humanity is a program in which people of all religious persuasions collaborate in building houses for the needy and the poor. One can easily detect in such a program how the people who engage in building such a house are doing it in the company of the poor who will later occupy that house. The religious persuasions of the participants do not stop anyone from engaging in a dialogue of action. The liberational character of the program is quite apparent from the way in which the people who occupy that house find dignity, freedom, and selfhood through the work of Habitat for Humanity. Another example is the way in which programs that aim at the "conscientization" of the poor and the marginalized express the kind of dialogue of action we are referring to. Christian and other social workers who work among the poor to enable them to take charge of their lives and engage in transformative political action are definitely involved in a dialogue of action that expresses cruciform responsibility, liberative solidarity, and eschatological mutuality in a grand manner.

The dialogue of theological exchange aims at promoting mutual understanding and respect among people of differing religious and secular traditions. This need not always be among the "specialists" of these traditions. Ordinary believers in these traditions could and do come together to share their faith with each other, thus deepening the understanding and enhancing the appreciation of one another's traditions. The Religious Friends Circle, which I have been a part of for several years in the city of Madurai, India, is a group of Christians, Hindus, and Muslims, and at times a few secularists as well, who meet for the exchange of their respective religious and theological traditions. It promotes mutual understanding and appreciation. For example, such dialogues help Christians to understand that the worship of images in the Hindu temples cannot be dismissed simply as idolatry. Hindus have a sophisticated understanding of the role of images in worshiping God. Similarly, such dialogues help Muslims to understand that the Christian view of the Trinity cannot simply be brushed off as polytheism. Hindus, as well, receive a fresh understanding and appreciation of the Christians' missionary vocation. The kind of mission we have outlined is furthered by these dialogues and conversations.

The dialogue of religious experience aims at spiritual growth and maturity that is achieved through sharing one's own spiritual resources with others, learning from others, and participating in the spiritual and liturgical practices of other religious traditions. This is a dialogue which is wrought with more theological and pastoral difficulties than the other three. Such a dialogue seems to imply a blanket affirmation of the equality of all religious traditions. Difficult questions arise, such as: Are we worshiping the one and the same God when we participate in the worship of other religious traditions? Is the church losing its prophetic and critical ministry when she encourages such dialogues of religious experience? Are we honest to ourselves when we assume that one can "participate" in the religious experience of the other? What about the uniqueness and finality of the revelation of God in Christ? These and many similar questions haunt us when we engage in the dialogue of religious experience. But these questions have not stopped Christians all over the world from engaging in such dialogues. It is, very often, those who participate in such dialogues who raise and address these questions. Both the Office of Interreligious Relations and the Pontifical Council for Interreligious Dialogue of the Vatican are engaged in consultations and conferences that address the issue of participation in the worship and spiritual practices of religious traditions other than one's own. The dialogue of religious experience, within our scheme, operates with the idea that solidarity and mutuality cannot be limited to discursive, day-to-day living, and sociopolitical realms alone. The call to solidarity and mutuality includes the religious, spiritual, and mystical realms as well, and rightly so.

Let me end the discussion of dialogue with the following remarks.

1. Dialogue is not merely a way of being "nice" to one another. Quite often, people who criticize dialogue and conversation in the missional context see dialogue merely as mutual affirmation, appreciation, and admiration. Conversation does involve a huge amount of mutual admiration and appreciation. One can detect this in every casual or serious conversation we have with another person or persons. But dialogue, in our usage here, means much more than that. It is *engagement* with the other, not simply pleasant *talk*. Genuine dialogue involves challenging, correcting, criticizing, and truly learning from one another.

2. Dialogue is witness even without an evangelistic agenda. Seeing dialogue as a preparation for the announcement of the good news is misguided. In dialogue one lives out the good news that God accepts all as God's own children and engages with continuous dialogue with God's own creation. In expressing our responsibility, solidarity, and mutuality with others in the various types of dialogue that we have outlined earlier, we are, in fact, making the good news present in the midst of our dialogue. It is a witness that simply expresses itself through "being there" with others in conversation, exchange, and action.

3. Dialogue does not preclude the announcement of the good news in Jesus the Christ. The kind of dialogue we are talking about is a conversation between people who are committed to their respective religious traditions. As Ariarajah expresses this so well:

We must begin with the affirmation that dialogue does not exclude witness. In fact, where people have no convictions to share, there can be no real dialogue. In a multilateral dialogue meeting in Colombo, one of the Hindu participants rejected any idea of "levelling down" religious convictions, and said that he had no interest in entering into dialogue with Christians who had no convictions about their faith. In any genuine dialogue authentic witness must take place, for partners will bear testimony to why they have this or that conviction.[33]

Authentic witness can and should happen in a dialogical situation. The only caution is that such witness should only take the form of *mutual* witnessing. It cannot be a one-way street at all.

In conclusion, what I have offered here is some of the ways in which certain areas of mission, such as evangelism, conversion, and so on, can be rethought and reworked within the theological framework that is offered in this book. I am aware that this is sketchy and needs to be looked at carefully and in a much more detailed fashion. There are also other areas which deserve our attention as well. Yet the one thing that is clear is that with the understanding of mission as cruciform responsibility, liberative solidarity, and eschatological mutuality, we can once again be renewed and revitalized to engage in the mission of the church today.

5

Rereading Our History

We began our exploration of a theology of mission in a wider circle of discussion than the ecclesial one—the mission of humanity—which meant that we could not begin our journey with the biblical and historical foundations for our understanding of Christian mission. Yet we need now to return to consider the Scriptures and the history of Christianity that have traditionally undergirded and even today sustain the Christian understanding of mission. In this chapter I will look specifically at the history of Christian mission over the last two thousand years. "Mission over the last two thousand years?" you ask. Yes, it is indeed a formidable task to trace and reread our missionary history. Because it is impossible even to begin to cover the entirety of this history in such a brief format, allow me to begin by mentioning a few considerations and methods that will help us to engage in a brief rereading of our missionary history without going into the many details of all the periods and places.

First, I propose to organize this chapter around several "models" of mission in the history of the church. These models are not arranged in chronological order, although one may detect a certain overall movement from the early church to the present time. Each model finds some kind of expression in almost every period of history in the life of the church. I will be illustrating each of the models with events and persons from differing periods of Christian history.

Second, I depend mostly on illustrative examples from the history of Christianity in India. This is not, in any way, to imply that Indian Christianity is a normative or highly typical case. Rather, it is a history with which I am more familiar than with others, and it seems to provide a rich variety of examples for most of the models that I discuss in this chapter.

Third, one of the problems we face here is the fact that the materials that provide us with information on the church's expression of mission through the ages are all written from a perspective that equates mission with the spread of Christianity. Therefore, our sources offer us events and trends in the *expansion* of Christianity throughout the world rather than a portrait of the various ways in which the *mission of the church* has been understood and practiced. Of course, these sources discuss these various models of mission mostly in the context of the expansion of Christianity. I would argue that expansion of Christianity is but only one model of mission among many, though a dominant one in the history of the church. One of the standard volumes on the history of mission is by Stephen Neill, titled *A History of Christian Missions*.[1] It is a comprehensive account of the history of mission, seen mostly from the angle of the spread of Christianity. The very use of the word "mission" in the plural in the title of the book suggests such a perspective. It is a history of *missions* and not *mission* as such. Both Neill and other mission historians do that. One exception to this is the volume by Timothy Yates, who limits himself to the twentieth century and organizes the history of mission under several models of mission.[2] Therefore, I take the historical accounts for what they are and weave a few models out of those histories to help us to understand how our history has been a history of varying—and at times intriguing—models of mission. Now let us look at the models.

1. Mission as Kerygmatic Presence

This is one of the earliest models of mission in the history of the church. The church in the New Testament saw itself as just being a community of faith at a given place. Look at the account of the early church at the end of Acts 2. The life of the church is described as the early disciples' being present in their society in an intentional and prophetic way. "Being sent"—the meaning of the term "mission"—was practiced more as "being" than by "being *sent.*" After all, the first few chapters of Acts do not describe much *going* at all. The disciples were where they were in intentional and specific ways. As one notices, the marks of this community were *kerygma, koinonia, diaconia,* and *marturia.* They preached the good news when occasions arose or when demands were made on them to explain their faith in Christ. The preaching of Peter in chapters 2, 3, 4, and 10 is all on the basis of an invitation or a demand from the people to explain the specific character of the disciples' presence in their midst. Thus, I call the mission of the early Christians "kerygmatic presence" because it was their way of living out the kerygma they announced. This kerygma was made real first by their *koinonia* (fellowship). "They devoted themselves to the apostles' teaching and *fellowship,* to the breaking of bread and the prayers. . . . All who believed were *together* and had all things in common" (Acts 2:42-44, italics mine). Second, the kerygma was lived out in their practice of *diaconia* (service). Peter's healing of the lame man in the temple (Acts 3) and the collection of offerings for those affected by the famine (Acts 11) are some of the ways in which they lived out their kerygma. Third, the kerygma was made concrete in their witness in word to be followed by martyrdom. That is what is meant by the term *marturia,* which can be translated as both witness and martyrdom.

The missionary journeys that are narrated in the Acts of the Apostles are themselves expressions of this kerygmatic presence. Being led by the Spirit, the evangelist Philip stands on the road from Jerusalem and witnesses to an Ethiopian minister. Being led by the Spirit, Paul and Barnabas journey to several cities of that region. In each place they live for a considerable amount of time and exercise their kerygmatic presence. Paul stayed in Ephesus for two years while he was in mission there. The account of Paul's mission in Philippi is an excellent example of the way in which Paul and others practiced their kerygmatic presence (Acts 16). They went about their daily living in that town, and when they came across the slave girl who was possessed by a spirit of divination and held captive by her owners, Paul exorcised her. When they met Lydia during one of their regular meetings near the river, they shared the good news of Jesus the Christ with her, and she and her family accepted the Christian faith. Lydia invited them to her home to stay with her for as long as they had planned to stay in Philippi. The emphasis in this account is clearly on local presence rather than on the business of sending and going.

Such a model of mission has been kept alive in differing ways by churches throughout their history. The Eastern Orthodox churches have, for example, been in the forefront of maintaining this model of kerygmatic presence as their primary one for missional practice. The Orthodox position views the liturgical, spiritual, and communitarian life of the local Christian congregation as the locus of mission. Liturgy is never seen merely as a gas station where one gets one's tank of spiritual energy filled up to be able to go out in mission. For the Orthodox, the liturgy, especially the "divine liturgy" (the eucharist), is itself mission.[3] The historic document prepared by the Orthodox Advisory Group to the World Council of Churches Commission on World Mission and Evangelism refers to the eucharistic liturgy as a missionary event and goes on to say:

> The eucharistic liturgy is the full participation of the faithful in the salvation brought about by the incarnation of the divine Logos and through them into the whole cosmos. . . . The liturgy is our thanksgiving for—and on behalf of—the created world, and the restoration in Christ of the fallen world. It is the image of the kingdom; it is the *cosmos* becoming *ecclesia*.[4]

Not only the Orthodox churches but other churches as well often see their mission as kerygmatic presence. Commenting on the prevalent model of mission from 1950 to 1960, Timothy Yates points to "presence and dialogue" as the primary model of that period. He highlights the work and writings of Max Warren, Stephen Neill, and Kenneth Cragg as those that advocated the idea of mission as presence.[5]

The idea of presence has also been dominant in the ways in which the modern missionary movement and churches today view the idea of *inculturation*. The gospel needs to be allowed to take its own root in the soil where it is sown. Here is a view that sees mission as a processive event in which the gospel slowly and steadily takes root in local situations, transforms those situations, and in the process gets transformed itself. Two famous examples of such attempts at mission as incultura-tion are Robert de Nobili, a Jesuit missionary who worked in South India during the seventeenth century,[6] and Father Vincent Donovan, who worked among the Masai Tribes in East Africa.[7]

2. Mission as Martyrdom

One of the hallmarks of the early church is that right from its very birth on the day of Pentecost, the church had to face persecutions. We read about the glorious beginning of the church in Acts 2, and from Acts 3 onward we come across several instances of persecution. Stephen is martyred, leading to a diaspora of the early disciples (Acts 7:54–8:3). Then comes the slaying of James, the brother of John, by King Herod (Acts 12:1-5). This is followed by the arrest of Peter and by Paul's frequent experiences with persecution during his missionary journeys.

Under the Roman government other persecutions of the early church took place. There were ten organized persecutions of Christians over a period of roughly three hundred years, from 64 C.E. to 305 C.E.[8] These persecutions started with Emperor Nero and ended at the time of Emperor Diocletian. Suffering and martyrdom became the chief modes of bearing witness to the power and meaning of the gospel of Jesus the Christ. It also gave a sense of identifying oneself with the crucified Lord. For example, in recording how Peter and John were flogged in the Council by the Jewish leaders and released, Luke, the author of Acts, had this to say: "As they left the council, they rejoiced that they were considered worthy to suffer dishonor for the sake of the name" (Acts 5:41). Suffering and persecution were seen as missionary obedi-ence *par excellence*. As church historians are fond of saying, the blood of the martyrs became the seed of the church, and the church grew in pro-portion to its persecution. Though the persecutions had ended by the time of Emperor Constantine, more situations of suffering arose during the period of the Muslim expansion into Europe. Suffering and mar-tyrdom became supreme expressions of missional existence.

This linkage of mission and martyrdom has stayed with us through the centuries. Even today missionaries are seen as potential martyrs. The history of the missionary movement during the last three centuries is filled with cases of persecution and suffering of Christians and Christian converts. Even in a nation like India, which is dominated by the most accommodative Hindu faith, there were sporadic, and at times sustained, instances of persecution. The development of Christian settlements and villages in the southernmost part of India was mainly due to the missionaries' attempt to protect the early converts to Christianity from Hindu persecution.[9] One can draw parallels to this from every continent.

The kind of cruciform responsibility that is required of Christian mission means that one could face suffering and persecution. The Christian gospel is a political gospel, and it leads to the questioning and challenging of the existing political and social arrangements in the society in which it is preached and practiced. The earliest confession of Christians, namely, "Jesus is Lord," is a political statement. It is especially highly political in a setting in which the political order promotes and sustains the lordship of Caesar. No wonder early Christians were persecuted. They were, in a way, following their Lord, who was killed on the cross as a political criminal. Similarly, when the gospel of Christ invited the untouchables of India to accept the Christian faith and thus regain selfhood, dignity, and pride, it was making an explosive political statement. Such a statement had occasionally triggered sporadic persecutions.

If mission involves solidarity with the poor for the liberation of all, it may provoke the anger of the rich and the powerful. When Paul healed the woman possessed with a spirit of fortune-telling, her owners saw that act as a threat to their power and authority. So they dragged Paul and Silas away and put them in prison (Acts 16:16-24). Mission that aims at the liberation of the oppressed does lead to suffering and martyrdom. Thus on the account of liberative solidarity, Christian mission ends up as martyrdom.

There is also a problematic side to the view of mission as martyrdom. It can lead to what one might call a "martyr-complex" among Christians. Martyrdom comes to be seen as the norm for an effective mission, rather than as one possible consequence of mission. Often the people in our churches think of missionaries as undergoing undue and unbearable suffering in the places where they are engaged in mission. Most often the missionaries who work in Asia, Africa, and Latin America are imagined to be marching toward martyrdom every minute of their life. In some cases, this may be true. But it is also the case that most missionaries enjoy their work among people who love them, receive them with affection, and offer the satisfaction of working for God. Such a "martyr-complex" sees people of other religions, cultures, and nations as our enemies and most often enemies of God. The kind of solidarity and mutuality that we propose is not possible in that kind of approach to people of other traditions and cultures.

3. Mission as Expansion

The model that I want to expound here is just the opposite of what we examined in the last section. This model came into prominence when the large-scale persecutions of early Christians had ended. The Edict of Milan (313 C.E.) by Emperor Constantine changed the situation of persecutions to a setting in which Christianity was bestowed with royal favor. Every attempt was made by Constantine to stabilize his empire through the building up of the Christian church. It was Constantine who called the first ecumenical council for the purpose of settling divisions among Christians over issues of doctrine and practice. He encouraged the construction of big church buildings, known as basilicas, with great pomp and glory. Constantine's mother, Helena, was involved in the recovering of relics connected with the life, ministry, death, and resurrection of Jesus. Constantine declared Sunday as the weekly holiday in 321 C.E. He humanized criminal law on the basis of Christian principles. Clergy and bishops were elevated to powerful positions. Thus Christianity came to be the most favored religion of the empire.

Once Christianity secured for itself a place of both comfort and honor, the view of mission came to be altered. Mission was no longer bearing witness in the midst of suffering and martyrdom; rather, it was now promoting the already favored religion of the powerful, such as the emperors. This led to a new understanding of mission as *expansion*. The expansionist program happened in two ways. The first was political, with European kings promoting the Christian cause. For example, St. Augustine of Canterbury was sent by Pope Gregory the Great in 596 C.E. to England where he was received by the King of Kent. Right from the very beginning the mission to England was backed by royal favor and support. Royal favor was a great boon to the growth and expansion of the church.

But this was true not only of the medieval period but of the modern era as well. The Roman Catholic missionaries to the New World had the blessings of the Spanish and Portuguese rulers.[10] Bartholomew Ziegenbalg, the first Protestant missionary to India, was sent by the King of Denmark in 1706 to land in the Danish colony in South India.[11] One can narrate several more examples of this kind. During the colonial expansion of the West into the continents of Africa and Asia, political patronage was offered to missionary work. Of course this was not true of all the mission movements during the colonial days. There were moments when the missionary movement and the colonial expansion could not go hand in hand. But most often the two helped each other. Discussing this "unholy" alliance between missionary expansion and colonialism, David Bosch points out that while the Western missionary enterprise was compromised by its association with colonial powers, there was also a "persistent minority" who "withstood the political imposition of the West on the rest of the world."[12]

There was a second aspect to this view of mission as expansion. The expansionist view promoted a militant view of mission as well. The birth and rapid spread of Islam into Europe created the setting in which this militancy in the Christian understanding of mission first developed. Islam and its rapid spread became a threat to Christianity. By 715 C.E., Spain, Syria, Palestine, and Persia were under the rule of Muslims. In 846 C.E., Rome was attacked and plundered by the Muslim forces. By 902 C.E., Sicily was conquered by the followers of Islam.[13]

In such a situation, mission came to be understood in militant terms. Thus were tragic and dark pages of Christian history opened. Western Christians saw their mission as military invasion against the Muslims of their day. From the eleventh to the thirteenth centuries, there was a series of wars called the Crusades (the wars of the cross). These wars were seen as attempts to recover the Holy Land from the hands of the Muslims and block their further expansion into Europe. The effects of these eight Crusades on the mission of the Church were disastrous. Discussing the consequences of the Crusades, Neill points out that they permanently injured the relations between Eastern Orthodox and Western Christians; that they sowed seeds of bitterness between Christians and Muslims, the harvest of which we reap even today; and that they lowered the "moral temperature" of Christianity.[14] Of course the Crusades were not meant to be missionary enterprises. Yet they brought a significant element of militancy into the life of the church.

Even before the Crusades, the militant character of expansionist mission could be seen in the way in which European kings saw their wars with neighboring kingdoms as part of their Christian mission. For example, King Charlemagne's campaign against the Saxons was his way of expressing the extension of the Christian religion. Saxons who refused to become Christians and accept baptism were by law condemned to death by the sword.[15] Conversion to Christianity was woven into many peace treaties, and even into royal marriages as well.

Today one would be hesitant to view mission as this type of militancy. But militaristic imagery and language has not fully been exorcized out of the vocabulary of Christian mission. Hymns, writings, and speeches continue to use militaristic imagery, which promotes the idea of mission as expansion in subtle ways. The kind of cruciform responsibility that we have put forward brings a strong theological critique to such militant understanding and practice of mission. Similarly, our idea of eschatological mutuality will not allow us to see others simply as enemies of the gospel who must be conquered and subdued.

4. Mission as Monastic Service

The monastic movement within Christianity began in Egypt with the work of St. Anthony of Thebes (251–356 C.E.). It was, to begin with, an expression of the deep spirituality of the desert fathers and mothers who, in and through ascetic life and practice, found their lives and the lives of those who came in contact with them enriched and blessed. Individual monks left the life of the cities and towns, moved to deserts, lived in solitude, and practiced austere spiritual disciplines. In this early period, the monastic movement was limited to and dominated by individual ascetics. At this point it had not taken a "missionary" turn. But soon the monastic movement entered its second stage, in which monks came to live in groups and communities (although these were not yet the clearly defined "religious orders" such as the Benedictines, Dominicans, and Franciscans, who would come later). With this turn from individual to group life, the monastic movement began also to take on a missionary agenda.

The Irish monks were the earliest of missionary monks. As early as 563 C.E., St. Columba arrived in the island of Iona and established a monastery. From this monastery monks were sent to Scotland and other places. Iona became the center of Celtic Christianity.[16] The Irish monks were followed by several other groups of monks in the years that followed. Their missionary tasks were marked by two features. First, the monks lived with the rural folk and served them, mainly because of the location of the monasteries in rural areas. Second, because of such close connection with the village folk and their religious traditions, these monks developed the vernacular cultures and languages. For example, Cyril and Methodius translated the Bible and the liturgies into the Slavonic language, though later these translations were banned.[17] Such well-known monks as St. Francis of Assisi (1181–1226), St. Dominic (1170–1221), and their followers were great missionaries in their service to the people among whom they lived and worked. Thus the ministry of the monks among the people led to the vision of the mission of the church as monastic service.

The view of mission as monastic service received a big boost when Ignatius Loyola (1495–1556) founded the Society of Jesus in 1534. The renewal within the Roman Catholic Church during the time of the Protestant Reformation led to a renewed interest in the missionary task of the church, which in turn produced Ignatius Loyola's establishment of the Society of Jesus. In addition to their magnificent work in the field of education, the Jesuits were pioneers in many forms of missionary work and continue to be so even to this day. Francis Xavier and Robert de Nobili, who pioneered into India and did yeomen missionary service, came from this monastic tradition. I am citing the Jesuits only as illustrative of the development of the idea of mission as monastic service. There were, and still are, several other religious orders that promote this view of mission.

One of the positive elements in this view of mission was that the monks and nuns were able to express solidarity with the poor and the oppressed in a manner that was much more sustained and powerful than what the laity—who were burdened by their own mundane, "secular" duties—could have done. They also had the time, energy, and spiritual discipline to engage in sustained missional activity, as opposed to the kind of "hit-and-run" evangelism that I referred to in the previous chapter. Most of the religious orders worked among the rural folks and among the poor. They were able to concretize the church's mandate "to bring good news to the poor."

One of the drawbacks of this model of mission, however, was that mission became the work of the specialists. This model robbed the church of its ownership of mission as a central part of its life, relegating the mission of the church to its monastic branch alone. It denied the individual Christian and individual congregations or parishes their mandate to *be* in mission.

5. Mission as Conversion of Heathens

Webster's Third New International Dictionary gives the following two meanings for the term "heathen." First, a heathen is "an unconverted member of a people or nation that does not acknowledge the God of the Bible." Second, a heathen is "a person whose culture or enlightenment is of an inferior grade." If a heathen is a person of this kind, then surely such a person needed to be converted and brought up to a superior culture. The Christian church has often, here and there, perceived those outside the church in this fashion. But viewing the mission of the church in terms of converting the heathens became a much more dominant model during the modern missionary movement of the last three centuries. A historic document that operated with this model of mission was William Carey's booklet entitled *An Enquiry into the Obligations of Christians to Use Means for the Conversion of the Heathens*, written in 1792.[18] The aim of this writing was to stir and motivate Christians in the West, especially in England, to use their resources for engaging in missionary work overseas. In this booklet, Carey describes the inhabitants of other parts of the world, very specifically those who do not have a written language or a literary tradition, as the "poor, barbarous, and destitute of civilization." Though this document is dated in the eighteenth century, the missionary attitude toward non-Western peoples that is reflected here has stayed with the church for centuries. Even today, there are Christians who view people of other cultures and other religious traditions as "heathens."

One can see how the sociopolitical and economic situation in the world of the eighteenth and nineteenth centuries would make this model of mission possible and sustainable. The colonial expansion of the West appeared to establish the supremacy of Western culture and religion (Christianity) by its very existence. The missionaries themselves fell prey to the prevalent culture of Western superiority, even though as persons they were totally dedicated to their missionary task and to a creative understanding of mission itself. William Carey himself was one of the greatest missionaries of the nineteenth century, and the marvelous service he did for the people of India does not go unrecognized in India by Indians themselves. Yet his own view of non-Western peoples was colored by the prevailing colonial ethos. Moreover, not all missionaries from the West operated with such a view of others, even when they used the phrase "heathen" to refer to the non-Western peoples. For example, the first Protestant missionary to India, Ziegenbalg, recognized the worth of the so-called heathens. He wrote:

> I do not reject everything they teach, rather rejoice that for the heathen long ago a small light of the Gospel began to shine. . . . One will find here and there such teachings and passages in their writings which are not only according to human reason but also according to God's word.[19]

Though there were exceptions such as Ziegenbalg and others, the dominant perspective of this model is to view the non-Western peoples as inferior and therefore to be converted to Christianity.

Such a view had its own effect on the way in which conversion to Christianity was understood. Conversion meant a dramatic cutting off from one's own culture and religion and an adopting of Western ways of living and acting. For example, Christian converts, both Roman Catholic and Protestant, in many parts of India were expected to take on biblical and Western names. My family is an example of this practice: my father's name is Melchizedec, my mother's Grace Janet, my brother's William, and mine Thomas. Quite a few of the converts were encouraged to change their dress, their ways of wearing their hair, and their food habits. Of course, the converts did not take on Western ways in every aspect of their lives. The same Indian Christians who took on Western names and dress code did not give up caste rules or marriage practices. But the tragedy of it all was the way in which Christian converts began to devalue their own culture, language, and rituals in light of the Western Christian ways of doing things.

Viewing mission as the conversion of heathens also led to a highly negative view of religions other than Christianity. Other religions were often seen as enemies of God. They were viewed as those that should be annihilated and abolished. Here again, one needs to make qualifications. There were missionaries who viewed other religions with understanding and appreciation. Kenneth Cracknell, writing about theologians and missionaries in the period from 1846 to 1914, offers us a vision of eight missionaries and five theologians from this period who viewed other religious traditions with understanding and thus practiced "justice, courtesy, and love."[20] Even in the midst of such courtesy and love, however, the mission of the church has been dominated by a negative view of other religions and cultures. From the theological standpoint advocated in this book, this view of other religions is due a severe critique. If mission is exercised in a spirit of eschatological mutuality and liberative solidarity, one cannot help but develop an appreciative and courteous view of other religions.

6. Mission as Mission Societies

The emergence of the modern Protestant missionary movement in the eighteenth century ushered in an era of the founding and maintaining of mission societies by the various Protestant churches in the West. The pervasiveness of mission societies during this period can be seen in the following impressive list of organizations:

- The Society for the Propagation of the Gospel (Anglican, 1701)
- The Church Missionary Society (Anglican, 1799)
- The Mission Society (English Baptist, 1792)
- The London Missionary Society (1795)
- The American Board of Commissioners of Foreign Missions (Congregationalist, 1810)
- The American Baptist Missionary Board (1814)
- The Berlin Society (1824)
- The Basel Mission (1815)
- The Danish Missionary Society (1821)
- Missionary societies in France (1822), Sweden (1835), and Norway (1842).

What the Roman Catholics were able to achieve with regard to the mission of the church in the wider world was achieved by the Protestant churches by their Mission Societies. For Protestants, mission came to be seen as the work of the Societies.

There were several positive features that came out of this emergence of Mission Societies. The Protestant churches throughout the world moved into an increased consciousness about the missional task of the church. Mission became a household word during the eighteenth and nineteenth centuries. This had an influence on churches in the non-Western world too. For example, the Christians in the area of Tirunelveli in South India began Mission Societies under the leadership of Bishop Azariah of Dornakal. The Indian Missionary Society of Tirunelveli (1903) and the National Missionary Society (1905) were founded with indigenous leadership and local resources.[21] Though people quite often understood mission as overseas mission, the awareness about the missionary character of the church was heightened by this model of mission. This model also meant an efficient way of utilizing the resources of the local churches for world mission.

There are, however, three problematic elements in this model of mission. First, mission came to be associated with Mission Societies to the extent that the local congregations or parishes at times failed to be in mission in their local situations through what I have earlier called "kerygmatic presence." People in local congregations fulfilled their missionary calling more by offering support (financial or otherwise) to the Mission Societies than by engaging in acts of mission themselves. Second, mission came to be seen as a *program* rather than as a way of being a Christian in any situation. Such a programmatic understanding can, and quite often does, rob people of the joy of engaging in "random acts of kindness." Once it is viewed as a *program*, mission is something only full-time missionaries can do. Third, mission of the church was mainly understood as "overseas" mission. Even though most Mission Societies had a "Home Mission" wing attached to their programs, most people saw mission as something that is carried out in faraway lands. This has continued to be the dominant view in many of the churches throughout the world.

7. Mission as Education

Establishing schools, colleges, and other educational institutions has been one of the main activities of the missionaries all along, especially during the last three centuries. One can detect the same trend in the monastic movements of the early period of the church and the scholastic movement during the medieval period of the history of the church. Some of the well-known missionaries of the modern missionary era, such as Alexander Duff, a Scottish Presbyterian missionary who pio-

neered in the task of higher education in India, saw educational efforts
as the most significant part of the missionary agenda. Of course, the
type of education was that which had developed in the West over a
period of several centuries.

Though most missionaries agreed on the importance of education in
the missionary task of the church, there were varied understandings as
to why and how the educational service should be offered. Some envi-
sioned education as a tool for winning converts to Christianity. Among
these, some saw the setting in the schools and colleges as a fertile ground
for teaching the Bible and thus the announcement of the gospel to young
students. Others saw education as a preparation for the gospel. What
they meant was this: Once "non-Christians" were offered Western education, they would be changed in their ways of thinking. Thus they
would be convinced of the superstitious and irrational character of their
own religions and convert to Christianity. For example, John Murdoch,
a Protestant missionary in India, published a booklet titled *Siva Bhakti
with an Examination of the Siddhanta Philosophy: An Appeal to Educated
Hindus* in 1902.[22] In this book he examines the beliefs and practices of a
group of Hindus in South India and hopes that any "educated" Hindu
will be easily and readily convinced of the superstitious character of
Hinduism and turn to Christianity. He ends the book this way: "May the
reader, instead of confirming by his example, his ignorant countrymen
in their degraded superstitions, take part in the glorious work of turning
them to the worship of the one true God, their rightful Lord, their
Father in heaven."[23] Thus education was seen as a tool for converting
people from their traditional religions to Christianity.

Some others saw the educational program of the mission societies as
simple and straightforward expression of the Christian duty to love one's
neighbor. Education is a liberating process; it is a process of widening
one's horizon and understanding of the world. Therefore, Christians who
have had the privilege of education are called upon to share their educational resources with those illiterate and disadvantaged peoples of the
world. It does not matter much whether those students who are enrolled
in the schools and colleges administered by the mission agencies decide
to become Christians through baptism or not. David Bosch refers to the
missionary awakening in Great Britain during the period from 1698 to
1815 as that which was motivated by the text: "For the love of Christ
urges us on" (2 Cor. 5:14).[24] One may say that the same text was the

inspiration behind those missionary educators who saw their educational task simply as an extension of the love of Christ. There has also been the view that education would instigate a rich ferment with the religious traditions of the students, and that in turn would bring reformation and renaissance within other religious traditions. One can safely say, for example, that some of the leading Hindu reformers of the nineteenth and twentieth centuries in India were partly inspired by the Western education they had received in Christian schools and colleges. Raja Ram Mohan Roy, Vivekananda, Gandhi, and Radhakrishnan belong to this group of reformers. This is not only true of India; one can find similar persons and trends within other regions and religions as well.

Finally, some see education as a process of conscientization. This is a model of mission that has gained significant attention in recent decades. Since the publication of the book *Pedagogy of the Oppressed* by Paulo Freire,[25] churches have come to understand their educational task in creative ways. Freire and others have brought to light the political and economic dimension of education, and have demonstrated how education can mean seeing one's potential for change and transformation. This leads to viewing mission as "educating" or "conscientizing" the poor and the oppressed for liberation. Such mission is undergirded by a vision of mission as liberative solidarity. I know of a group of Christians in South India who are involved in an educational program that aims to offer literacy, health, and political education to the poor in the rural areas through the use of well-known proverbs. For example, the proverb "Only a crying baby gets milk" is used to introduce certain alphabets that make up the word "mother," to bring an awareness about the importance and the right mode of breast-feeding babies, and to raise the people's consciousness to their need to give voice to their rights within the given political setting.

Viewing the mission of the church as an educational enterprise has, in a way, coincided with the theological vision of cruciform responsibility and liberative solidarity. Except for the view of education as a manipulative tool for conversion, the other models of education need to be continued in our context today.

8. Mission as Joint Action for Justice and Peace

The church from its very beginnings had placed justice and peace as high priorities in its missionary agenda. An incident in chapter 6 of the book of Acts is one example of the way in which the church had to face the issue of justice. "The Hellenists complained against the Hebrews because their widows were being neglected in the daily distribution of food" (v. 1) — clearly an issue of justice and peace. The church did not fail to address this issue, and consequently established a structure that would ensure justice for all. Thus the seven, including Stephen the martyr, were chosen to serve. A matter of interest in that story is that the church met together as a whole community and engaged in a joint action. "And the twelve called together the whole community of the disciples" and made the decision to institute the order of the seven (v. 2). In the same manner of engaging in joint action, they addressed the needs of those who were affected by famine (Acts 11:29). A further example is the council (often referred to as the first ecumenical council) that met in Jerusalem to discuss the status of Christians who were not of Jewish religious background (Acts 15).

Such engagement in "joint action" has not always been the case with the churches throughout the world. Divisions arose among Christians, which led to the practicing of Christian missionary obedience in divisive and competitive ways. The modern Protestant missionary movement is known for its tragic dividedness. What is called the "Comity of Missions" operated, though not always successfully, among Protestant missionaries, dividing lands in the non-Western world among missionaries so that they would not clash with one another in competitive missionary programs. As Stephen Neill calls it, this principle had its own "absurdities and limitations." He writes:

> It could hardly be thought reasonable that the inhabitant of a village on one side of a small stream should be baptized not merely as a Lutheran but as a Danish Lutheran; and that his cousin on the other side of the stream should become a member of the American Dutch Reformed Church. Geography, not conviction, became the basis for denominational allegiance.[26]

The area of South India where I come from is rampant with stories of severe competition and rivalry among the missionaries of the Society for the Propagation of the Gospel and those of the Church Missionary Society, both of the Church of England. Thus in the early period of the missionary movement, there was quite a bit of competition among the various mission agencies. The Comity of Missions was one way of addressing this issue.

Several missionary conferences during the later part of the nineteenth century and then in the early twentieth century were efforts by missionaries all over the world to come to terms with this division and work towards unity. Edinburgh 1910 marks a clear and important stage in the move toward mutuality and cooperation. The two World Wars also forced the churches to think in terms of cooperation because of the global character of our problems. In this manner the missionary movement laid the foundations for the Ecumenical Movement of this century, which had as one of its dramatic moments the founding of the World Council of Churches in 1948.

Such an effort at unity was not simply on a global level. It permeated the local church situations as well. More and more Christians began to see the need to work together for justice and peace in their local situations. Today, in most areas of the world, the credibility of the gospel and the effectiveness of programs that promote justice and peace demand this ecumenicity among the practitioners of Christian mission. This has also led to an increased amount of cooperation among the Mission Societies of the mainline Protestant churches and between Roman Catholics, Orthodox Christians, and Protestants. This ecumenical spirit has led to viewing mission and missionary programs as expressions of the catholicity of the church. If one takes the catholicity of the church seriously, then churches throughout the world need to work in partnership with one another for a credible witness to the transforming power of the gospel in situations of injustice and conflict.

In today's world there is a larger ecumenicity that is demanded of Christians as well. As we have noted and discussed through the previous chapters, we are in a wider circle of discussion, which calls for an extended partnership and a broader understanding of cooperation. People who belong to religions other than Christianity and those who lead secular-based lives become partners with Christians in humanity's attempt to set its house in order. No single group can work in isolation and expect any significant social and economic transformation in the "global village" of today. We have already discussed this idea in the last chapter when we examined the relation between mission and dialogue. It is sufficient to add that the theological framework we are engaging in our project here supports and promotes such a joint action for justice and peace in today's world.

What I have outlined so far are eight models of mission that give us a glimpse of the history that has informed and continues to inform and shape our understanding of mission today. One learns from this history how the small steps of missionary obedience taken by Christians throughout the world have helped to concretize and put into practice the gospel of Jesus the Christ in profoundly meaningful and helpful ways. These definitely were steps in the direction of the coming Reign of God, which is a community of justice and peace. At the same time, our history also exposes the demonic and destructive distortions of the Christian mission. It shows how in the name of Christ and Christian mission peoples and nations have been subjugated and devalued. Thus, a rereading of our history in this manner alerts us to the dangers of an overenthusiastic, thoughtless, and uncritical exercising of our missionary mandate. It also calls us to articulate new visions and engage in new forms of mission in today's world. When one begins to imaginatively construct a novel and relevant vision of mission, one is quite often muzzled and silenced by particular ways of reading the Christian Scriptures. New theologies of mission are dismissed as unbiblical and contrary to the "word of God" and denied a full hearing. What is the way out of such a bottleneck? How shall we read the Bible today in articulating a relevant theology of mission? This is the question we address in the next chapter.

6

Reinterpreting the Bible

When we began our exploration into a relevant theology of mission for today, we decided not to start with a discussion of the biblical foundations for mission. This was done in order to engage in a conversation wider than an intra-ecclesial one. Since the Bible is the book of and for the Christian community of faith, and since our purpose was to seek a theology of mission that takes the pluralistic context in which mission takes place as its starting point, it made sense to begin in a way other than appealing to the biblical view of mission, because the authority of the Bible is one that those of other religions either do not recognize or recognize in a way that is different from that of Christians. But at this point in our discussion, it is right and fitting that we go back to the Bible and see how one would understand and interpret the Bible for the understanding and practice of mission.

In chapter 2, I mentioned how most often evangelicals saw the so-called Great Commission in Matthew 28:16-20 as the organizing center for their biblical view of mission; whereas the ecumenicals, especially those operating within the framework of liberation theologies, found the so-called Nazareth Manifesto in Luke 4:16-20 to be their "canon within the canon." I made note of this mainly to highlight the fact that we all read the Bible selectively and with an eye to the context in which we find ourselves. Since the Bible is a library of books, one chooses materials within this library in two specific ways. First, certain texts and passages attract our attention because of the questions and issues raised by the context in which we find ourselves. For example, the nineteenth century missionary movement, while it was growing and spreading into every nook and corner of the globe, found the Great Commission to be attracting the attention of missionary theologians and interpreters. Similarly, in the situation of oppression and exploitation in the countries of Latin America, the liberation theologians' attention was attracted to the Nazareth Manifesto in Luke's Gospel. Thus, the demands of our context can draw us to particular texts within the Bible. Second, it is not we who choose texts within the Bible at all times; there are times when certain biblical texts jump out of the pages of the Bible, so to speak, and demand our attention. Martin Luther's discovery of the text from Romans that changed his life and the life of the church is one such experience. Those who are engaged in the preaching ministry of the church are quite aware how, in the process of preparing the sermon, one is gripped by certain texts and passages as though for the first time. Thus the selection of biblical texts is a process in which our reading of our context and our openness to the leading of the Spirit come together in a dialectical manner.

In this chapter I will attempt to present, first, a broad biblical vision of mission in light of the way I read the Bible, in the context of a wider circle of conversation, and with an openness to the surprises with which the Spirit may confront us. Second, I will take up one particular set of texts that have been very often employed as a warrant to dismiss the kind of theology of mission that we have developed here.

1. A Biblical Vision

As an introductory remark, I want to mention that I am engaging in a reinterpretation of the biblical view of mission more as a theologian than as a scholar in biblical studies as such. This is because my own training has been in the field of systematic theology, and not out of disregard for biblical scholarship. I value the work of biblical scholars in my own constructive theological work very highly, and I am aware that one can engage in a thoroughgoing exegesis and hermeneutics of the biblical documents to arrive at the biblical views of mission. There are two major works in recent years that offer us a critical overview of the biblical views of mission. Those are *The Biblical Foundations for Mission* by Donald Senior and Carroll Stuhlmueller,[1] and part I of David Bosch's volume, *Transforming Mission*. While I am informed by these two works, what I am attempting in this chapter is a reimagining of the biblical vision of what it means to be in mission. The two concerns that we had raised in the introduction, namely, the widening of the circle of discussion and the crisis of confidence, are particularly operative in my choice and interpretation of biblical materials.

Let me begin with the Hebrew Bible. Of course, we cannot engage in a detailed study here of the ideas of mission in the Hebrew Bible for obvious reasons. We had earlier noted how the Bible is a "library" of books and how the variety within the Bible will not allow any easy summation of ideas found there regarding mission. Therefore, what I offer are some dominant themes with regard to the understanding of mission. Two other words of caution are necessary at this point. First, the history of the theological use of the Hebrew Bible among Christians is to be noted with utmost seriousness. The use of the term "Old Testament" to refer to the Hebrew Bible has often led to anti-Semitic interpretations of its contents, with demonic consequences for the relations between Christians and Jews. The type of interreligious conversation that undergirds our theological project here demands that we recognize this difficulty and approach the Hebrew Bible in much more sympathetic and appreciative ways. For this reason it is unfair to call it the "Old" Testament. Perhaps one could refer to it as the "First" Testament. The best option would be to refer to it by its own name, the Hebrew Bible. Such a naming acknowledges the integrity of the Jewish religious tradition and helps us recognize, at the same time, the foundational role that the Hebrew Bible plays in Christian life, thought, and practice. I also want to acknowledge that I am reading the Hebrew Bible as a Christian and not as one who belongs to the Jewish religious tradition. Therefore, while I respect the integrity of the Hebrew Bible, my interpretation still operates with certain limitations that are necessary for any biblical hermeneutics that takes the portrait of Jesus the Christ in the Gospels as the key and norm.

Second, the Hebrew Bible contains within itself three aspects of mission, namely, the mission of God, the mission of humanity, and the mission of the people of Israel. These three are closely interrelated and cannot be understood in isolation from one another. At the same time, one needs to recognize that these three are mixed up together in such a way that unless we take them apart, delineate them, and examine them, we may not arrive at a clear understanding of mission as presented by the Hebrew Bible. We should also bear in mind that the mission of the people of Israel is set within the context of a larger framework, namely, the mission of God and the mission of humanity. The fact that the book of Genesis precedes the book of Exodus shows that the particular calling of the people of Israel is within the context of God's calling of the universe into existence and God's covenant with the whole of creation. To be more specific, the call of Abraham follows the calling forth of the universe into existence by God. The covenant with Noah precedes the covenant with Abraham. The interweaving of the mission of God and the mission of the people of Israel is a bit more complex than what I have outlined so far. In a way, the wider and universal mission of God is articulated on the basis of the specific call of God to the people of Israel to be the "light unto the nations." In other words, Genesis, though it precedes Exodus, is written from the perspective of Exodus. Given these two words of caution, let us enter into the world of the Hebrew Bible and begin with the mission of God as it is outlined there. We will examine the mission of God and the mission of the people of Israel initially and return to the theme of the mission of humanity at the end after we have explored the New Testament's views on mission as well.

The Mission of God

The Bible opens with the "missionary" act of God in creation. "In the beginning . . . God created the heavens and the earth" (Gen. 1:1). The word "mission," which means "being sent," could be translated as "going forth" as well. Creation is itself an act of mission in the sense that God "goes forth" in the creative activity. Of course there is no "space" for God to be going forth to. It is all God in the beginning. Therefore, one might say that there is a going forth of God to God. God's word *(Logos)* goes forth and returns to God in the act of creation. God said "Let there be light" and there was light. God's word goes forth, brings light into being, and returns to God. Here is God in God's own missionary journey! We should recognize the missionary journey of God here. K. C. Sen, the Indian theologian, in his lecture on Trinity refers to it as "the Still God," "the Journeying God," and "the Returning God."[2] Sen, of course, uses the idea of a movement or journey in relation to the idea of Trinity. But we can see that it is quite relevant, as well, to the missionary character of God's creation of the universe. Thus the opening pages of the Bible present us with a God who, in God's own inner essence, is a "missionary God." God's creativity goes forth in bringing life into existence, sustaining an overall context for that existence, and enabling it to flourish and fill the earth.

If one sees God's creation of the universe as God's missionary activity, one is immediately struck by the next missionary act of God. In describing the creation of the world in six days, the writer of the first chapter of Genesis ends the story with the creation of humanity. The creation of humanity is described this way:

> So God created humankind in [God's] image, in the image of God [God] created them; male and female [God] created them. God blessed them, and God said to them, "Be fruitful and multiply, and fill the earth and subdue it; and have dominion over the fish of the sea and over the birds of the air and over every living thing that moves upon the earth." (Gen. 1:27-28)

It is very enlightening to see how God's missionary act of creation is followed immediately by God's sharing God's mission with humanity. God creates humankind in God's own image—that is, with the creativity that God shows forth in creation—and asks humans to share in that creativity. The image is the power and capacity that God has bestowed upon humans to be creative—in other words, to "be fruitful and multiply." In creating humans in the image of God, God shares God's own mission with humans. God's mission is a **shared mission**. "Image of God" is the symbol of God's sharing of God's mission with humanity. It is not just with men that God shares; God shares with both men and women because the image of God in the human is also expressed by God's creating humans as male and female. Male and female God created them, and shared God's mission with the whole of humanity.

After all, we were right in beginning our theological exercise with a discussion of *missio humanitatis*. God has shared God's mission with humans in creation, and therefore all humans are created to be in mission; thus it is possible to engage in a dialogue on *missio humanitatis* as beings created in the image of God. We will pick up on this theme of *missio humanitatis* later. Mission, as God wants it to be, can happen only when it is shared with others. One may raise an objection here. Did not this sharing of mission by God with humans happen in the beginning of Creation, when humans were, as it were, in paradise? What about the situation of humans after the Fall in Genesis 3? Does God share God's mission with "fallen" humans too? As we read through the story of the Fall and the events that follow, it is clear that God continues to share God's mission with humans. Humans are still given the task of continuing their creative mission even in the midst of a "cursed" situation.[3] The story of Cain, the story of God's cooperative mission with Noah, and others are indicative of the fact that God continues to share God's mission with humanity even in its sinful state. The account of the flowering of civilizations, as recorded in Genesis 4:19-22, is a grand picture of God's sharing God's creative work with humans. Farming, art, and technology are some of the creative expressions of this mission that humans share with God.

Quite often in our history, we have not engaged in *shared* mission. We noted how the missionaries of the modern Protestant missionary movement were engaged in rivalry and competition. It is only in the ecumenical movement of this century that Protestants (and others as well) have learned what it means to be engaged in shared mission. As I mentioned earlier, this sharing of our mission is not only to be done with other Christians but with people of all religious traditions, people of secular persuasions, and other living beings in the universe as well.

God's mission, which was manifested in God's creation of this universe, continues in and through God's affirming of life in all its varied forms. God's mission is a *life-affirming* mission. God is a God of life, and therefore God affirms life. Even after the Fall, God becomes the preserver of life on earth and protects Cain from being murdered (Gen. 4:13-16). Later, in the story of the Flood, we see that the mission of God to preserve life is active again. Timothy Findley's novel *Not Wanted on the Voyage* is an interesting fictional account of Noah's story. The author presents God as being tempted to give up God's mission and destroy the whole world. But God overcomes the temptation, and through a sharing of God's mission with Noah, preserves life. Interestingly, God preserves life in all its variety and multiplicity. One may even say that at this point God's life-affirming mission becomes an *ecological* mission (Gen. 8:20). God promises to continue God's ecological mission by entering into a covenant with Noah. Not only humanity but all of creation is preserved. Here again there is an invitation to the whole of humanity to share God's mission in the Noachic covenant. God shares God's mission with the whole of creation, especially with humans, and affirms life and all that sustains life.

If God's mission is one of affirmation of life, we humans, even though fallen, need to be highly critical of any mission efforts that do not affirm others but rather end up annihilating them. This should be true of our relationship with other humans and other human communities as well as our relationship with nature as such. Our relationship, within the framework of mission, with humans and other beings in the universe is one of affirmation and preservation of life.

A shared mission invariably leads to a mission of *suffering*. God suffers along with creation in God's engagement in the mission of affirmation. God suffers; God becomes vulnerable. Though there are passages in the Hebrew Bible in which God appears as a mighty and tribal warrior, the overall and dominant picture of God is that of a sufferer. Why is this so? God's mission is a shattered mission because in sharing God's mission with humans God has allowed the possibility of humans' shattering God's mission. Humans can distort and destroy God's mission. In such a situation, God suffers, of course, along with humans. The book of Hosea is a supreme example of this aspect of God's mission. God cries out in total vulnerability:

> How can I give you up, Ephraim? How can I hand you over, O Israel?
> How can I make you like Admah? How can I treat you like Zeboiim?
> My heart recoils within me; my compassion grows warm and tender.
> I will not execute my fierce anger; I will not again destroy Ephraim.
> (Hos. 11:8-9)

Thus, God's mission is a mission of suffering with those who are the marginalized of this earth; and in thus suffering with those who suffer, God brings liberation and freedom to all. In this sense, God's mission in the Hebrew Bible is a *liberative mission*.

The Mission of the People of Israel

It is in the light of this universal and loving, shared and life-affirming, and suffering and caring mission of God that we need to look at the mission of the Jewish people. When we use a phrase such as "the mission of the people of Israel," we need to observe two elements of caution. First, we need to remember that we do not limit ourselves to the contemporary misunderstanding that defines mission purely in terms of "overseas mission." The only "overseas" missionary we encounter in the Hebrew Bible is Jonah, and it is a story where Jonah becomes a missionary to the people of Nineveh, and they in turn become missionaries to Jonah in an indirect way. So if we understand mission merely as overseas mission, the people of Israel do not have a mission in the pages of the Bible. If we look at this issue from a broader perspective, we will be convinced that the people of Israel do have a mission and that it is expressed in several ways in the pages of the Bible. Second, I am not including a discussion of the contemporary nation of Israel in our understanding of the mission of the people of Israel. Though some may view such a discussion as an integral part of Israel's mission, it is sufficient, for our purposes, to limit our discussion to biblical times.

The central motif in the mission of the people of Israel is their freedom from bondage in Egypt. That is what sustains the mission of Israel. Therefore, the mission of the people of Israel is to live a life of gratitude to God for the liberation that God has offered to them in Egypt and continues to offer in their history thereafter. The keeping of the commandments is their way of being engaged in a mission of gratitude to God. That is why, for example, the Ten Commandments begin with this sentence: "I am the LORD your God, who brought you out of the land of Egypt, out of the house of slavery; you shall have no other gods before me" (Exod. 20:2). After such an introduction, the other commandments follow. Therefore the mission of Israel is a mission in gratitude.

This mission of gratitude is not only celebrative of the liberation that God offered earlier and continues to offer them. It is also a mission in which they themselves are invited to share in God's mission of liberation. An excellent illustration is the commandment to keep the Sabbath holy. While the account of the Ten Commandments in Exodus 20 cites God's resting on the seventh day as the rationale for observing the Sabbath, the account in Deuteronomy clearly points to the liberating gratitude as the reason for the observance of Sabbath. "Remember that you were a slave in the land of Egypt, and the LORD your God brought you out from there with a mighty hand and an outstretched arm; therefore the LORD your God commanded you to keep the sabbath day" (Deut. 5:15). Israel's gratitude is expressed in giving a day of rest to the workers and the resident aliens in remembrance of their liberation from Egyptian slavery. Similarly, the celebration of the jubilee year is both an expression of gratitude and a direct engagement in the liberation of the poor and the landless (Lev. 25:8-55). Thus the mission of the people of Israel is a mission in gratitude expressed through acts of liberation and freedom.

In the understanding and practice of this liberative mission of gratitude, the people of God in the Hebrew Bible experience several tensions. They find themselves between polarities in a situation that cannot be resolved simply by choosing one of the poles. Both need to be kept in a tension. Hence we mention that they had to go through "tensions." Let me list a few and discuss them.

The people of Israel experience a tension between what one might call the religiocultural and the sociopolitical expressions of their gratitude. The religious rituals, rules, and regulations were given as a way of expressing gratitude. The temple, the sacrifices, the festivals, the observance of several rules regarding food, and others are all expressions of their mission of thanksgiving. At times, these take a prominent place over the sociopolitical issues of justice and peace. Maintaining justice and peace in their own community is also an expression of the mission of gratitude. In the tension between these two modes of expressing one's gratitude, the people of Israel quite often tend to choose one of the poles, namely, the religious rituals, at the expense of a life of justice and peace. One of the major tasks of the prophets in the Hebrew Bible was to invite people to a holistic mission that includes the religiocultural expressions of gratitude as well as the sociopolitical ways of establishing and maintaining justice. The prophets Amos, Micah, and Isaiah very clearly invite people to such a holistic mission. For example, God speaks through Amos this way:

> I hate, I despise your festivals, and I take no delight in your solemn assemblies. Even though you offer me your burnt offerings and grain offerings, I will not accept them; and the offerings of well-being of your fatted

animals I will not look upon. Take away from me the noise of your songs; I will not listen to the melody of your harps. But let justice roll down like waters, and righteousness like an everflowing stream. (Amos 5:21-24)

Similar sentiments are expressed by other prophets as well.[4] The people of Israel are called to keep both expressions of gratitude—ritualistic and liberative—in tension and thus engage in holistic mission.

The second tension is between an ethnic nationalism and a liberative universalism. The people of Israel saw themselves as the chosen and elected ones of God, called to be the light to the nations. Isaiah proclaims God's word of assurance to the people of Israel this way: "I have given you as a covenant to the people, a light to the nations" (Isa. 42:6). This idea was often interpreted as a great privilege and an awesome responsibility. This gave the people of Israel a great sense of responsibility to be diligent in their mission of gratitude and liberation. Yet at times the idea of election conjured up ethnic and nationalistic feelings in contrast to a liberative, universalistic view of their mission. The idea of election came to have a negative influence. Separatist and exclusivistic tendencies developed. Here again the prophets were keen to bring the people to a sense of a holistic mission. By speaking about King Cyrus as the chosen of God, Isaiah raises the consciousness of Israel to the true understanding of election (Isa. 45:1-19) and brings back a sense of universalism. The whole book of Jonah aims to resolve the tension between ethnic nationalism and liberative universalism. God, who cares about the liberation of the people of Israel, is equally concerned with the well-being of the people of Nineveh. Similarly, Amos awakens people to a realization that God has been about God's mission of liberation among people other than the Hebrews, such as the Philistines and the Syrians (Amos 9:7). The book of Psalms, as well, celebrates God's liberative involvement with the whole earth and all its nations (see Pss. 67:4 and 96:2-13).

The third tension is between the understanding of mission as conquest and of mission as suffering. While the Hebrew Bible is filled with militaristic imagery of God's mission and the mission of the people of Israel, there are strong and powerful portrayals of the mission of the people of Israel as that of a mission of suffering. The servant songs in the book of Isaiah portray this aspect of suffering in a clear and picturesque manner. The people of Israel themselves are the suffering servants who should be willing to be "despised and rejected by others," to be "oppressed" and "afflicted" "like a lamb that is led to the slaughter, and like a sheep that before its shearers is silent" (Isa. 53:3, 7). The mission of the people of Israel is both conquest and suffering.

To conclude our discussion of the idea of mission in the Hebrew Bible, let me highlight a few points. God, in God's very nature, is a missionary God. God goes forth in love and compassion in God's creative activity, in God's affirming and liberative view of life on earth, and in God's own suffering with and for the poor and marginalized of the earth for the liberation of all. God never engages in mission alone; God invites God's creatures, especially the human beings, to share in God's mission. Within this framework of God's own mission, the people of Israel are invited to practice their mission in gratitude. Such gratitude is to be expressed both through its liturgical, ritualistic practices and through its serious engagement with issues of justice and peace in larger society. Such an engagement is not simply for conquest and success, it is also expressed through suffering and failure. It is a mission that knows no boundaries in terms of nations, class, race, or gender. All are invited to be in mission with God.

The Mission of Jesus

With the discussion of the mission of Jesus, we move into the New Testament. We need to note right away that there is a dialectical relationship between the Hebrew Bible and the New Testament. This means that there is both a continuity and a discontinuity between the two. Any discussion of mission in the New Testament cannot but take seriously into account the Hebrew Bible's articulation of it. Jesus, as a Jew, was informed and shaped by the Hebrew understandings of what it means to be in mission. At the same time, the New Testament makes a critical departure from the Hebrew Bible in making the events surrounding and including Jesus as normative for its understandings of mission. Something novel has entered the tradition when Jesus is made the central and normative figure. Such a dialectical understanding of the relation between the Hebrew Bible and the New Testament can save us from two dangers. On the one hand, it saves us from any anti-Semitic sentiments and interpretations of the New Testament. On the other, it allows us to recognize and own the novelty that enters the scriptures with and through the life, ministry, death, and resurrection of Jesus the Christ.

Another preliminary remark is also needed at this point. Just like the Hebrew Bible, the New Testament does not give us a single understanding of mission. It presents us with the mission of Jesus, the mission of the disciples, and the mission of humanity in a grand tapestry of various views of mission. For the sake of clarity, we need to separate these and look at each of them carefully, and recover the tapestry once again to capture the vision of the New Testament. We shall initially examine the mission of Jesus and the mission of the disciples, and toward the end consider the mission of humanity.

It is quite appropriate at this point to begin with the mission of Jesus as we delve into the views of mission in the New Testament, because the church's mission is founded on the mission of Jesus. It does not mean that the mission of Jesus *is* the mission of the church; rather, Jesus' mission is foundational for any explication of the mission of the church. That is why a little later we will examine the mission of the disciples separately from the mission of Jesus. Now to the mission of Jesus. We cannot discuss in detail every aspect of the understanding and practice of mission that Jesus had. We will highlight only a few salient features.

As we read the pages of the New Testament, it is apparent that Jesus saw himself as *sent* by God. He spoke of his ministry as that of one who is *sent* by God. For example, he says: "Let us go on to the neighboring towns, so that I may proclaim the message there also; for that is what I came out to do" (Mark 1:38). This sense of a "missionary" vocation is also reflected in Jesus' sending his disciples as "missionaries." He says, "As the Father has sent me, so I send you" (John 20:21). There are several other places in the Fourth Gospel where Jesus speaks of his being sent by God into the world. Such a sense of "missionary" vocation in Jesus is something that is debatable. For example, the question of the "messianic secret," which is mentioned in the Synoptic Gospels, may raise problems as to determining the self-consciousness of Jesus with regard to his vocation. However, one can confidently claim that the Gospel writers present Jesus as one who is *sent* by God, and he in turn sends his disciples. Based on this one may see Jesus, his life, and his ministry as the enfleshing of the mission of God. In a sense, one can say that in Jesus of Nazareth the mission of God "became flesh and lived among us."

The Gospel accounts of the life of Jesus clearly portray a Jesus who lived with a tension between ethnic nationalism and liberative universalism, as we had explained in our exposition of the views of mission in the Hebrew Bible. As Senior and Stuhlmueller write:

> Reports of Jesus' encounters with Gentiles are relatively rare, and there is strong evidence that he concentrated his mission first and foremost on the community of Israel. Matthew 10:5 and 15:24 present Jesus as explicitly rejecting activity among the Gentiles, and he is highly critical of the proselytizing activity of the Pharisees (cf. Matt. 23:15).[5]

Though there is a clear focus on the Jewish community in the mission of Jesus, Matthew does not fail to report the moments of tension. The conversation with the Canaanite woman in chapter 15 is clearly indicative of this tension. In this story, Jesus comes out on the side of liberative universalism. Matthew also describes the universal character of Jesus' mission in his post-resurrection sayings. Senior and Stuhlmueller discuss the various ways in which scholars have tried to take account of this tension, and we do not go into them here. It is sufficient to note that the Gospels portray Jesus as one who lived with this tension yet opted for universalism. This is true of the Lukan pericope (often referred to as the Nazareth Manifesto), where the proclamation of the jubilee is understood by the hearers in ethnic and nationalist terms, and Jesus goes on to broaden it to liberative and universal terms through his narration of the stories of the widow of Zarephath and Naaman the Syrian (Luke 4:16-30).

What is the nature and character of Jesus' mission, as it is recorded in the Gospels? If one can summarize the nature and purpose of the mission of Jesus in a single phrase, it will be "the Reign of God."[6] In earlier translations of the New Testament, the phrase "Kingdom of God" was used. We are aware of the patriarchal and monarchical character of the phrase "the Kingdom of God" and of its destructive possibilities in relation to human relationships. Therefore, we shall consistently use "the Reign of God." The idea of the "Reign of God" brings together in a marvelous way all that Jesus stood for. In other words, it gives us a way of understanding the major thrust of Jesus' mission. The Reign of God is expressed and lived out in the ministry of Jesus through his teaching, performance of miracles, acts of healing, and everyday activities, such as eating and so on. When we look at the whole ministry and life of Jesus, we can recognize some significant elements of the idea of the Reign of God. Let me mention a few aspects of this Reign as it surfaces in the Gospels.

One of the marks of this Reign is universality or inclusivity. In using the metaphor of a feast to describe the character of the Reign, Jesus points to the inclusivity of this Reign. All are invited to the feast, and no one is left out.[7] It is not only presented as an inclusive feast in the teachings of Jesus, it is lived out by Jesus in his eating and drinking with the so-called sinners of his day, namely, the prostitutes, tax-gatherers, and publicans.

Another hallmark of this Reign is that it is a community of forgiveness. All are forgiven by God, and all are called to forgive one another. The story of the prodigal son in Luke 15 exemplifies this character of the Reign of God. It is a reign of peace with justice. Here forgiveness is seen as that which goes beyond questions of justice, while affirming and maintaining justice. Yet another mark of the Reign of God is the health and prosperity that it brings. There is healing and there is food for all. The healing miracles are, as in the words of the author of Fourth Gospel, signs of this health and prosperity. So are the miracles of turning water into wine in Cana and of the feeding of the five thousand with five loaves and two fish. Such a Reign of God is here and now, and it is yet to come. There is a tension between its being here right now present among us and its coming to fruition and fullness in the eschaton. That is why the parables of the Reign of God have both stories of a present reality and portrayal of the judgment at the eschaton. One is called to live in the interim between the "here and now" and the "not-yet." The not-yet character of the Reign enables us to question and challenge all present forms of order, relationship, and culture.

In outlining the features of the Reign of God, Jesus never fails to point out the way of the cross as an important part in the ushering in of this Reign. His teachings on the Reign are always accompanied by his foretelling and describing his coming suffering and death. This, perhaps, is one of the reasons why the Gospel writers gave such a prominent place to the Passion narratives that one could call the Gospels "Passion narratives with extended introduction."

As one can see, the mission of Jesus was one of announcing, acting out, and suffering for the Reign of God, which, while present among humans, awaits consummation at the eschaton. Thus was the mission of Jesus.

The Mission of the Disciples

We noted that Jesus lived with a sense of mission and sent his disciples on a mission as well. If the Christian church is a community of disciples of Jesus the Christ, then it is sent on a mission by Christ, as Jesus sent his disciples during his day. In light of this, one can say that what the church is doing today is enacting the mission of the disciples of Jesus rather than the mission of Jesus himself. This distinction must be made and maintained because the post-resurrection community of disciples was not simply doing what Jesus did. Theirs was a mission different from the mission of Jesus. This distinction happened because of certain shifts that took place as the mission of Jesus was transferred to the disciples. Let me mention a few of the shifts. First of all, Jesus is no longer merely the "missioner" or the initiator of mission, but he becomes the central content of the mission. In other words, the one who came announcing the Reign of God becomes a part of the content of the Reign of God. The announcer becomes the announced. Jesus the Christ has himself become the central core of the good news. He is no longer simply the announcer of the good news. He *is* the good news. Thus mission becomes a matter of discipleship.[8] This is one of the major reasons why one cannot simply define mission today as acts of charity, justice, and care. Mission includes the naming of Jesus as the sign of the Reign of God. If we rightly understand the close relation between Jesus the announcer and Jesus the announced, we will be invariably led to see mission in a much more holistic manner that what is normally done in Christian communities.

The second shift that took place is the move from "Reign of God" to "Church in Society." Bosch quotes Alfred Loisy as writing, "Jesus foretold the reign and it was the Church that came."[9] An Indian Christian theologian, Chenchiah, puts this in a much stronger language. He writes:

> Christianity took the wrong gradient when it left the Kingdom of God for the Church . . . Christianity is a failure because we made a religion of it instead of a new creation . . . The Church arrested the Kingdom when Peter added 3000 unto them—a fatal day for the Kingdom and a glorious day for the Church. . . . When the Holy Spirit became a distant reality and then a dogma, when Jesus went to heaven and did not return, we thought of a Church and built one.[10]

It is not fair to the early church if we see this shift purely as something negative, as Chenchiah seems to imply. The development of the church as an institution was a necessary and healthy development. What we are maintaining here is that a shift happened in the perception of what it means to be in mission when the idea of church took precedence over the Reign of God. One can see how during the times of persecutions the early church could only think in terms of the Reign; but when peace arrived and Christianity became a religion with royal patronage, the church took precedence over the Reign.

The third shift was a definite process of universalization. Though Jesus lived with the tension between nationalism and universalism, and though he had resolved most of it, the disciples had to go through the same tension in their mission. We see this in the book of Acts, beginning with the story of Peter and Cornelius in Acts 10. Then come the missionary journeys of Paul and Barnabas from chapter 13 onward that open the doors of the church for the Gentile Christians. The inclusion of Gentile Christians in the community of faith was not an easy process. It had to be discussed and resolved in the first ecumenical council of the church in Jerusalem (Acts 15). The decision in this first council was a historic one because it publicly and powerfully acknowledged the universal character of the mission of the church. Once such a "universalization" had taken place, the christological thinking of the church developed in a much larger, universal, and cosmic framework. For example, Paul's letters to the Colossians and the Ephesians bring out the cosmic character of the gospel.

The fourth shift is the increase in the political character of Christian mission. Though Jesus died as a political and religious criminal, the political character of Christian mission takes shape over a period of time as we read the story of the early church in the Acts of the Apostles. It is enlightening to see how the story of Acts begins with the religious center of the Hebrew people, Jerusalem, and ends with Rome, the political capital, where Paul is held prisoner. The shift from Jerusalem to Rome is symbolic of the way mission became a subversive and at times revolutionary task. No wonder the people in Thessalonica shouted "These people who have been turning the world upside down have come here also" (Acts 17:6). The very proclamation "Jesus Christ is Lord" was a subversive proclamation at a time when Caesar was Lord.

The Mission of Humanity

In discussing the mission of God, of the people of Israel, of Jesus, and of the disciples, we touched upon some of the aspects of what the Bible sees as the mission of humanity. Now we need to bring them all together to articulate the mission of humanity as understood by the biblical writers. Having been created by God, in God's own image, all humans have a mission, and they share that mission with God. By bestowing this on all humanity, God has, in a way, "democratized" the idea of mission. Mission belongs to all. All humans are called and sent to be creative, life-affirming, liberative, and compassionate in their relationships with other humans and with other living and nonliving beings in the universe. All humans have the responsibility "in the garden of Eden to till it and keep it" (Gen. 2:15). A responsible relationship with the environment that sustains human life is required of all humans.

As we noted earlier, this relationship of God with humans in a shared mission is not limited to the life in paradise; it continues after the fall of humanity as well. God enters into a covenant with Cain, and later in a highly dramatic way enters into a relationship of shared mission with Noah. The covenant with Noah encompasses the whole of humanity, not just the chosen people of God—Hebrews in the Hebrew Bible and Christians in the New Testament. God's call to peoples and nations to walk in God's way is not limited to one people or one nation. The call goes out to all, Hebrews, Philistines, and Syrians as well (Amos 9:7).

Furthermore, all humans are invited to be involved in the *liberative* mission of God. God's offer of liberation is not limited to one people or one nation. It is offered to all humans in every part of the world. Such a universal offer of liberation comes with a call to engage in the act of liberation in one's own setting. Here again there is a democratization of God's mission as it is shared with humanity.

Such a universal and liberative mission for all humans is again presented to us in the teachings and ministry of Jesus, especially in his vision of the Reign of God. All are invited to the feast of the Reign of God. Such a vision demands that we view the mission of humanity as that which is practiced in a setting of dialogue and engagement with one another. All bring their gifts to the feast, and in a sharing of all gifts, the mission is shared with God. Communities of conversation become the loci for the practice of the mission of humanity. In serious and com-

137

passionate engagement with one another, humans exercise their God-given mission. The Bible ends with a picture of the new creation, in which all the nations bring their honor and wealth into that city of God that has no walls or gates but is open to all.[11]

To conclude our portrayal of the biblical vision of mission, we have seen that the biblical vision of the mission of the church is undergirded by all the five elements mentioned herein, namely, the mission of God, the mission of the people of Israel, the mission of Jesus, the mission of the disciples, and the mission of humanity. None of these five can be taken in isolation to define the mission of the church. It is a creative and imaginative combination of these five that makes up the mission of the church today. One can see how this vision offers us a mission that is creative, life-affirming, shared, liberative, and celebrative, with the Reign of God as the eschatological community to which we as disciples of Jesus the Christ march in faith, hope, and love, together with the whole of creation.

2. Some Difficult Texts

The kind of biblical vision that we have presented here is quite often questioned and rejected on the basis of some particular texts within the New Testament. Since our vision here is inclusive of other peoples and their religious traditions, and since it is undergirded by the preeminence of dialogue and conversation, the two texts that are often quoted against this vision are John 14:6 and Acts 4:12.

> Jesus said to him [Thomas], "I am the way, and the truth, and the life. No one comes to the Father except through me." (John 14:6)

> There is salvation in no one else, for there is no other name under heaven given among mortals by which we must be saved. (Acts 4:12)

These two texts are often quoted to silence those who suggest a broader and wider vision of the Reign of God than the community of faith that is sustained by a public acknowledgment of Jesus Christ as the only Savior of the world. Of course, such a use of a text from the Bible, what one would call the method of prooftexting, is not a helpful way of employing biblical texts in understanding the mission of the church. But the fact that people do use these as proof texts to argue against any and every attempt at a dialogical and inclusive understanding of mission demands that we engage in a reinterpretation of these texts. In recent years many theologians, scholars, and pastors have had to wrestle with these texts to reinterpret them.[12] Let me mention a few possible reinterpretations, primarily of the Johannine text.

One way to interpret this passage is to recognize straightforwardly the nature of the Fourth Gospel. One may claim that John's Gospel is more a sermon on Jesus rather than a verbatim account of what Jesus actually said. Therefore, one can, without much difficulty, conclude that Jesus himself did not actually say these words. Instead it is the author who articulates the confession of his commmunity of faith and places these words in the mouth of Jesus. The Jesus of the Synoptic Gospels is one who never claimed anything for himself, much less his being *the* way, *the* truth, and *the* life. He was very reluctant to claim any title for himself. When the rich young man asked him, "Good Teacher, what must I do to inherit eternal life?" Jesus said to him, "Why do you call me good? No one is good but God alone" (Mark 10:17-18). In light of the evidence from the Synoptics, together with the recognition that the Fourth Gospel is a homily on Jesus, it is apparent to some that Jesus never said these words.

One may ask at this point, does this interpretation in any way remove the exclusivistic problem in the words attributed to Jesus? The fact that the author, representing the early church, claims that Jesus is the way, the truth, and the life, must be taken equally seriously whether Jesus himself said them or not. The author is one of the original witnesses to the events surrounding and including Jesus of Nazareth. Therefore, his words matter a great deal; and thus understanding these words as John's words does not in any way remove or tone down the exclusive character of this text.

Another way of reinterpretation is to ask the question: What is the setting in which Jesus spoke these words? Was Jesus answering the question as to how the disciples should relate to others in a society like ours? Did the disciples ask Jesus how they were to engage in mission in a wider circle of discussion like the one we find ourselves in? They definitely did not. The setting in which the Fourth Gospel was written is different from ours. It was a context in which Jewish and Hellenistic Christians were engaged in a process of defining themselves as Christians. The Jews and Greeks of that day were demanding from the early Christians some clarity with regard to their emerging Christian identity. Who are these people who claim Jesus as Lord? What is it that makes them different from the Jews and the Greeks? These were the questions that were in the forefront in the setting of John's Gospel.

Therefore, when Jesus claims that he is the way, the truth, and the life, we see an emerging definition of what it means to be a Christian. A follower of Christ is one who takes Jesus to be his or her way, truth, and life; and is one who opts for no other. It is true that such a singular devotion to Christ is what makes people distinctively Christian. If we remove John 14:6 from its original context and uncritically place it in today's context, to judge the destiny of all those people who are outside the four walls of the church would be to take it totally out of its context and derive conclusions that are not intended in that verse. Even today, for Christians, Christ is the only way, the truth, and the life. Such is the faith-affirmation of this text, and it is not necessarily followed by any exclusivistic claims about the salvation and destiny of others. In our theological exercise we have continued to claim that a Christian under-standing of mission has something unique and precious to offer to the enhancement of *missio humanitatis* that is a birthright of every human being in the world. But it can be offered only in the context of an equally strong affirmation of the universality of God's sharing God's mission with the whole of creation.

Yet another way to reinterpret John 14:6 is to begin with the following question: What is the editorial or redactive setting in which this text is placed by the author of the Fourth Gospel? This directive hermeneutical question can be answered in two ways. First, one may look at the editorial setting of the whole Gospel. The author begins the Gospel with a poem on the Logos (Word) put in a direction of under-standing the life, ministry, death, and resurrection of Jesus in the light of the portrait of Jesus as the enfleshing of the Logos. "And the Word became flesh and lived among us, and we have seen his glory, the glory of a father's only son, full of grace and truth" (John 1:14). Jesus who reveals the glory of God as the incarnation of the Word is the hero of the story here. This means that the one who is claiming to be the way, the truth, and the life is not simply a man called Jesus in first-century Palestine. It is the Word-made-flesh who is making this claim. The Logos is in the beginning with God and is God. It is this Logos who is the light of the world who enlightens every human being (John 1:9).

If the opening prologue invites us to view Jesus as the Word-made-flesh, then it would be proper to understand John 14:6 to mean that no one comes to God except through the Logos who enlightens everyone. Therefore, in our context of dialogue and engagement with people of all religious and secular traditions, John 14:6 simply means that God is accessible to all through God's own reaching out to humanity through the Logos; and Christians have come to recognize this outreach of God (or the mission of God, which is a universal mission) through the life, ministry, death, and resurrection of Jesus the Christ. Since God is always and everywhere in mission, reaching out to the universe in love and care, we need to engage in dialogue with others in order to come to fuller understanding and adoration of the mission of God.

Second, one may begin with the immediate editorial setting of John 14:6. We all know that the chapter divisions in the Fourth Gospel are not the author's own making. The author wrote the Gospel as a single, long, and continuous piece. The chapter divisions were done much later, not always with a clear and reasonable warrant. If so, we need to ask: Where does the incident that leads to Jesus' proclamation that he is the way, the truth, and the life begin in the author's own arrangement of the narratives? It is apparent that the conversation on the "way" begins when Peter asks in chapter 13, "Lord, where are you going?" Then the conversation follows this way:

> Jesus answered, "Where I am going, you cannot follow me now; but you will follow afterward." Peter said to him, "Lord, why can I not follow you now? I will lay down my life for you." (vv. 36-37)

While the conversation began with the question about the way, it shifts right away to something else. Peter makes this shift by sensing what the journey and the way are all about. By saying "I will lay down my life for you," he indicates that the theme of "way" and the theme of "death" are closely related in this conversation. As one can see in chapters 12 and 13, Jesus speaks out significantly about the impending death.[13] Thus the way that one is referring to here is the way of suffering and death. It is the way of willing self-sacrifice and suffering. Therefore, one can conclude that Jesus, in claiming "I am the way, and the truth, and the life," is actually referring to the way of self-sacrifice and suffering.

141

Such a reinterpretation would mean that the thrust of John 14:6 is not to make exclusive claims for the Christian faith as such. Rather it is to assert the centrality of what the cross of Christ signifies for the life of a Christian or Christian community. There is no other way to God, there is no other truth, and there is nothing more life-giving than self-sacrifice and suffering for the sake of others. One has already read in chapter 12 before getting to 14:6 the following proclamation by Jesus: "Those who love their life lose it, and those who hate their life in this world will keep it for eternal life. Whoever serves me must follow me" (vv. 25-26). This echoes what Jesus says in the Synoptic Gospels, namely, "Whoever does not carry the cross and follow me cannot be my disciple" (Luke 14:27). Jesus makes this point again in chapter 15, when he says "No one has greater love than this, to lay down one's life for one's friends" (v. 13).

What Jesus offers in this text is a picture of what it means to be his disciple. He points to the centrality of love and self-sacrifice in the life of a disciple. This is the way that a disciple should take, that is the truth that is revealed in the enfleshing of Logos, and that is the life that overcomes death. Jesus in this passage is not telling us about the mission of Christians in the context of a wider circle of conversation; rather he is pointing to the centrality of love and self-sacrifice as the only way to the heart of God, because God's heart is a wounded heart.

What I have offered here are some of the possible ways of reinterpreting John 14:6, a text that has been used, most often, to short-circuit the efforts to re-imagine a theology of mission that takes seriously into account the wider circle of discussion and *missio humanitatis*. One may engage in a similar reinterpretation of Acts 4:12. The context of this passage is the healing of a man near the temple pool in Jerusalem by Peter and John. This miraculous healing had raised a lot of questions in the minds of those who witnessed the miracle, and especially in the minds of those rulers and elders who were upset by the commotion that this incident had created. So they rightly ask Peter and John one of the most relevant religious questions of that day: "By what power or by what name did you do this?" (Acts 4:7). Peter's declaration of a universal and an apparently exclusive claim about the salvation in Christ Jesus came as response to this question. Peter declares that the healing of the lame man was done through none other than the power and name of Jesus. Interestingly, the word that is translated as "save" and "salvation" is a word that also means "heal" and "healing."

That means that Peter's declaration is precisely in relation to the healing that had happened and the name that had been used in and for the process of healing. We would be violating the integrity of the passage if we were to place it within the context of today and thus draw extremely exclusivistic conclusions.

Above all, one needs to ask: What is the overall vision that is presented to us by the Bible with regard to the mission of the church? Given the particularities and realities of our context today, what is the biblical vision that could undergird our participation in God's mission with others both within the human family and within the larger ecological family? In answering this question what we have done and need to do more is avoid getting hung up on a few isolated texts such as John 14:6 and Acts 4:12, and recapture the grand and holistic vision that the Bible offers to us. We have been engaged in such an interpretative exercise in this chapter. Such an engagement with the Bible has given us a picture of mission that, in the words of Jay McDaniel, has both "roots and wings."[14] Our mission is rooted in our experience of the flourishing and fulfillment in the Christian faith from its commitment to the centrality of the transformation that has been inaugurated in the life, death, and resurrection of Jesus the Christ. Our mission, at the same time, in its openness to the Spirit of God at work in the world, gets its wings to fly into unknown areas of service in adventuresome cooperation with the people of the globe and with the living and nonliving beings in this vast universe. It is in such a grand vision of missionary vocation that Christians are called to participate in and to celebrate the grace, love, and goodness of God and God's creation. In this sense, it is right to call it "the common task."

7

Motivating for Mission

One further issue needs our consideration. How does one motivate the people in our churches and congregations for the kind of mission we have sketched out? What are the resources from which one may draw inspiration and motivation for mission? There are at least three positions taken with regard to the task of motivating for mission. First, there are those who are so guilt-ridden by the excesses of the modern, especially Protestant, missionary enterprise of the last three centuries that they consider "mission" to be a mistake. One should note that these are not people who are unconcerned about the welfare of their neighbors both far and near. Nonetheless, they find the word "mission" and all that is associated with it so inherently triumphalistic and oppressive that they would not have any part in it. Such people would like to remove the "missionary" agenda completely from the life of the local church. I would argue that those who hold this view need to be confronted with a rereading of Christian history that, while recognizing the excesses, is able to show that Christian mission has done good to many a people in the world. Our own rereading in chapter 5 is one such exercise. Such a rereading would involve going back to the days when one's own ancestors embraced the Christian faith and analyzing how this had meant liberation, meaning, and fulfillment in their lives. It would also involve a careful listening to the "testimony" of people from various parts of the world who found the gospel to be a liberating force in their own histories. On the whole, one cannot approach the question of mission merely within the framework of Western Christians' guilt and dismiss it as irrelevant.

Second, some others find it hard to be motivated for mission due to the influence of postmodern thinking and the acute individualism of our societies. They find mission to be totally unnecessary. "Let each person have his or her own religion, faith, and culture, and we shall simply let each other alone and refrain from any engagement in mission," they say. Such a "benevolent indifference" is viewed as being more desirable than a confrontation with one another. If we engage at all in a dialogue with the other, it should be limited simply to coming to know and appreciate the religion and culture of the other, rather than in any way attempting to influence or change the other. One can question the underlying view of neighborliness that is limited to being "nice" to each other and that becomes, in fact, simple indifference to one another. As we discussed in chapter 4, Christians have "a story to tell to the nations," and it is a loving, neighborly act to share that story in humility and love. Moreover, we have argued all along that the world we live in today is such an interconnected and interdependent world that we simply cannot afford to ignore each other and still ensure justice and peace in our world. It is to be hoped that an awareness of the interconnectedness of all life will awaken people from their slumber of indifference.

A third group of people are those who are highly motivated for an engagement in mission but find that the kind of theology of mission that we have outlined here is inadequate and uninspiring as any strong motivation for mission. If all are in mission, and all are called by God to be in mission, what is so special and unique about Christian mission? If our sense of inclusivity calls for a certain amount of theological and soteriological universalism, why be in mission at all? These questions are generally raised by those who are motivated for mission on the basis of one or more of the following reasons. One of the leading motivations is this:

The driving motive of Christians in these years [of the modern missionary movement] was a passion for souls. With the vivid belief in the reality of heaven and hell, Christians sought to rescue people from eternal punishment and to open the door of heaven for them before it was too late.[1]

Some have operated with a view of having been chosen from among the people of the world to be the sole announcers and presenters of the good news in Jesus the Christ. As such, one is demanded to go on a mission because God has authorized one or one's own Christian community to engaged in such a mission. Some even operate with the idea that their own citizenship in heaven would be at stake if they did not "win souls for Christ." I remember one of the hymns of my childhood days that describes how one cannot meet God on the other side of Jordan if one is empty-handed, without having won any souls for Christ. The sudden and unexpected Second Coming of Christ is another motivation that is used to instill a sense of urgency in the missionary task of the church. These and other such motivations do not find a central place in the kind of theology of mission we have developed herein. So those who are motivated for mission with these reasons would invariably find our theology of mission to be sadly wanting in motivating people for mission.

How, then, shall one be motivated to engage in a mission of responsibility, solidarity, and mutuality? Are there powerful motivations for mission other than the ones we have mentioned earlier? Are there theological resources for inspiration and motivation? I believe there are. Let me highlight only a few of them.

1. Doxological Motivation

One of the primary motivations for mission is our adoration of God. Humans are created to glorify God; not only humanity but all of creation is created for praise and adoration of God. The psalmist writes, "The heavens are telling the glory of God; and the firmament proclaims [God's] handiwork" (Ps. 19:1). God invites all humans to enjoy bliss and joy in the adoration of God. While this is the overall context for the creation's relation to God, does this really offer motivation for mission? Yes it does. The idea of adoration as a motivation for mission is very much present in the context of the "sending" narratives within the Bible. Let me cite three examples. First, in the book of Isaiah we read about the "sending" of Isaiah on a mission to announce God's word of judgment to the people of Israel. It is very interesting to note that this "sending" happens in the context of an adoration of the glory and awesomeness of God. Isaiah writes:

> I saw the Lord sitting on a throne, high and lofty; and the hem of his robe filled the temple. Seraphs were in attendance above him. . . . And one called to another and said: "Holy, holy, holy is the LORD of hosts; the whole earth is full of his glory." (Isa. 6:1-3)

It is within this context of adoration and doxology that God addresses Isaiah and cries out, "Whom shall I send, and who will go for us?" Isaiah answers, "Here I am; send me!" Motivation for mission happens in the context of the adoration of God. The second illustration is from the narrative within the Gospels where Jesus sends his disciples on a mission. In giving them the instructions for their "missionary" journey, Jesus places the greatness and glory of God in front of the disciples. Jesus says, "The harvest is plentiful, but the laborers are few; therefore ask the Lord of the harvest to send out laborers into his harvest" (Luke 10:2). That which should motivate the disciples in their mission is the fact that God is at work, and God's glory is revealed in God's own sending of laborers. It is the recognition of the priority and sovereignty of God that is the motivating force in this narrative.

The third example comes from the Great Commission itself. In interpreting the Great Commission in Matthew 28:16-20, Mortimer Arias asks the question: "Is there anything in the Great Commission to indicate a motivation for mission?" Then he goes on to answer it this way:

> The answer actually appears right at the beginning of the passage, in the context in which the disciples receive the last command from the resurrected Lord: "When they saw him, they worshiped him." It was this "seeing," this experience of the living Lord that motivated them. . . . Worship is the most powerful means of conversion and evangelistic experience, if we look at it rightly and with the right expectations. It can also become a source of motivation and power for mission in the world, and if this is not happening, something is wrong with our worship.[2]

The motivation for mission comes, as rightly pointed out by Arias, from our worship of the living Lord. When we truly adore God, we feel "sent" into the world.

It is fitting to name this as "doxological" motivation, because the word "doxology" comes from the Greek word *doxa*, which means "praise," "honor," "splendor," and "glory." It is this doxological awareness that can be a great motivating force for mission. Of course, such a doxological motivation may not lead to "conquest," "winning of souls," and so on. It will, rather, lead to living out one's mission as the *celebration* of the love and splendor of God. The song of Mary, the Magnificat, begins with the adoration of God and moves on to talk about the mighty and liberative acts of God's mission in the world.

The kind of doxology that we are referring to is not limited to the glory and splendor of God as it has been revealed in the past or is present in our midst today. It is a doxology of hope as well. It is an adoration of God that waits in eager expectation of the revealing of the glory of God in end times. Since God, as we have described in the biblical vision in the last chapter, is a missionary God, adoration of God invariably leads to involvement in mission by those who adore God.

Another way in which this doxological motivation is articulated is through the phrase "loving gratitude." As we noticed in our exposition of the mission of the people of Israel, the people of Israel are motivated to engage in mission as a thankful response, or as an expression of their loving gratitude for what God has done for them by bringing them out of the house of bondage in Egypt. In discussing the practice of evangelism in the early church, Michael Green places "a sense of gratitude" as the foremost motive of early Christians to engage in evangelism. He writes:

> There can be little doubt that the main motive for evangelism was a theological one. These men did not spread their message because it was advisable for them to do so, nor because it was the socially responsible thing to do. . . . They did it because of the overwhelming experience of the love of God which they had received through Jesus Christ.[3]

An adoration of God leads to a profound sense of love for and gratitude to God, which in turn motivates us for engagement with others in mission. Paul expresses the same sentiment when he writes, "the love of Christ urges us on" (2 Cor. 5:14).

2. Christological Motivation

In the previous chapter, we attempted a reinterpretation of the text in the Fourth Gospel (John 14:6) in which Jesus the Christ claims that he is the way, the truth, and the life. This text has been, in the past and even today among several Christian communities, interpreted to mean that Jesus is the unique and final revelation of God and the savior of the world. Such a high view of the revelation and redemption in Jesus the Christ has provided strong motivation for Christians to engage in mission. Our reinterpretation of this text and the underlying christology that informs our theology of mission may appear as one which will sadly lack in its ability to motivate people to engage in mission.

We have used two words to describe the christological claim, namely, "unique" and "final." Quite often we use these two terms as synonyms. I want to look at them as two separate words. Christians claim that in Jesus the Christ one encounters a *unique* revelation of God, and experiences a *unique* offer of salvation. One need not argue too much to establish the uniqueness of Jesus the Christ. The gospel of Jesus the Christ is unique. It is unique in the manner in which it understands the human problem, in the way it portrays Jesus the Christ as the savior, and in the path of salvation it points to. It is unique indeed. Such a strong affirmation of uniqueness is great motivation for our engagement in mission. People all over the world have their religions, understandings of salvation, and various paths to salvation. They are not all the same. They are all individually different and distinctive. Such an affirmation of distinctiveness is absolutely necessary if one is keen to respect the integrity of each religious tradition. Once uniqueness is affirmed in this sense, then there is every reason that the Christian community needs to be engaged in mission. It has something *unique* to offer to the world, and it should offer it. Thus a strong assertion with regard to the uniqueness of Jesus the Christ can provide inspiration and motivation for an engagement in mission.

The word "final" is very different in meaning. In naming the revelation and redemption in Jesus the Christ as "final," one faces several theological and missiological difficulties. For example, such a view of finality makes the revelatory and redemptory act of God closed and boxed within the history of Jesus and the history of the Christian community. Beginning with the prophets of old, such as Amos, Isaiah, and Micah, the Christian community has been invited to move away from such "boxing" or "enclosure" of God's activity in the universe. Such a view stops the kind of conversation and dialogue that we have talked about even before it can start. The idea of "eschatological mutuality" that we have discussed demands of us that we handle the idea of finality with "fear and trembling." It has every possibility of becoming idolatrous and leading to what one might call "Christolatry." We need a christology that is disciplined by a pneumatology that recognizes the work of the Spirit in all parts of the universe, most often in unexpected places and communities. Thus we need to "exploit" the idea of uniqueness for a strong motivation for mission and speak of the finality of Christ only in eschatological terms.

3. Soteriological Motivation

In the past, especially during the modern missionary movement, an exclusivistic understanding of salvation has provided a strong motivation for Christians to engage in mission. Such an understanding of salvation operated with these four affirmations. First, all have sinned and lost their relationship with God. This means that there is no point of contact between God and humanity. Second, such a chasm between God and humanity implies that all human efforts to reach God and reestablish the broken relationship are in vain. Those efforts take us nowhere. At their best, they take us only to that which is not God, to an idol of our own making. Third, in Jesus the Christ God has reconciled humanity back to a loving relationship with God. This has been supremely achieved through Jesus' death on the cross and his resurrection on the third day. Fourth, anyone who believes in the name of Jesus the Christ, accepts baptism, and joins the Christian community of faith escapes condemnation and enjoys bliss with God here and in the hereafter.

These affirmations, when held together, divide the world and humanity into two clearly definable camps—one, those who believe in Jesus the Christ and thus are bound for heaven; and the other, those who do not and thus are on the way to hell. If such is the case, it is the duty of all Christians to rescue the rest of humanity from its speedy descent into hell. Such a vision of others evokes feelings of pity, sympathy, love, and concern for those who are lost; and those feelings definitely provide strong motivation for mission. Since every minute people all over the world are passing into eternity through death without knowing the name of Christ, Christians should feel the urgency and act in mission right away.

The picture of salvation that is painted in our work here is different. It envisions mission as a collaborative and dialogical work alongside of others for the transformation of the world. Such a vision is undergirded by a "sacramental" or "eucharistic" view of the universe. Creation, redemption, and consummation are all held together in the idea of the Reign of God. In such a setting, salvation becomes a eucharistic transformation of the whole universe. We outlined this transformation as personal, societal, and ecological transformation in chapter 5. Such an understanding of salvation does not create a dualistic picture of the "saved" and the "unsaved." It does recognize the universality of sin and the universal appeal of the salvation that is brought about by the life, death, and resurrection of Jesus the Christ. But it is not restricted to a picture of "our" rescuing "others" from the fires of hell. Rather, mission is an invitation to join hands with others in building a world of justice, peace, and ecological health.

Such a mission is motivated by the love of the neighbor, of course. But it is not a love that goes out to "rescue" because that neighbor is on the path to condemnation; rather, it is a love that recognizes a fellow traveler in the other, a fellow pilgrim in the neighbor, and a companion in humanity's journey toward well-being and fulfillment. Such a love looks at the face of the other and notices immediately the family resemblance, and embraces others and invites them to join the path toward the wholeness of creation.

4. Ecclesiological Motivation

In discussing some of the "questionable motives" in the task of evangelism, Eddie Fox and George Morris point to how at times Christians have been motivated by a desire to preserve the institution of the church.[4] Quite often, people envision the church as a megainstitution, and thus mission becomes the "program" for maintaining and preserving this institution. The reduction of evangelism to "membership drive" is an outcome of such a perception of the place and function of the church in the world. Thus, the way one perceives the church can lead to different types of motivations for mission.

Avery Dulles, in his well-acclaimed volume on the church, presents us with several types or models of the church as it is understood and perceived by the people in the church.[5] He presents the church as Institution, as Mystical Communion, as Sacrament, as Herald, as Servant, and as Community of Disciples; and goes on to explain what implications one might draw from each of the models for the life and mission of the church. One may find one or more of these models of the church helpful in motivating oneself for mission.

I want to highlight a model that we discussed in the rereading of our history in chapter 5. The church, as it begins its infancy in Acts 2, is one that is marked by *kerygma* (preaching of the message), *koinonia* (fellowship), *diaconia* (service), and *marturia* (witness and martyrdom). One does not find a "programmatic" motivation in the way in which the early church lived out its missionary obedience. To be a church is to be in mission. One does not need a separate motivation as such, one might say. Let the church be the church. Then, of course, it is and will be in mission. This truth has been expressed by theologians in several ways. Some would say that mission is the *ontological* vocation of the church. Mission belongs to the very being of the church. When one begins to perceive the church in these terms, then one finds ample inspiration and motivation to engage in mission.

5. Eschatological Motivation

The Christian theological tradition, through the ages, has depended on two portrayals of the end times, the eschaton. One is a picture of the end as a time of separation and eternal division—division between the believers and the unbelievers, between the sheep and the goats, between heaven and hell. Such an eschatological vision, together with the Second Coming of Christ, has offered strong motivation for people to engage in mission. There is also another picture of the end within the Christian theological and biblical tradition. It is a vision of unity—of all things coming together in Christ. Both these pictures are available within the biblical writings. For example, there are parables of the Reign of God in the Gospels that portray such a final division of humanity into two camps. The Judgment Day is presented as the time when this ultimate and eternal division will take place.[6] At the same time, there are other parables that speak of a feast where all come together—the younger son and the elder son, the sinners and the righteous—into one new creation of God.[7]

Two defining categories in our explication of mission—liberative solidarity and eschatological mutuality—operate with an eschatology of unity or coming together rather than an eschatology of division. Could this offer any motivation for mission? It can, and for this we need to turn to the biblical and theological understanding of the role and place of the Holy Spirit in divine economy. The idea of the Holy Spirit as the bringer of the eschaton is very clearly presented in the New Testament. It is the Spirit that is groaning with the whole of creation for the eschatological community of justice and peace to arrive here on earth. As Paul expresses it:

> We know that the whole creation has been groaning in labor pains until now; and not only the creation, but we ourselves, who have the first fruits of the Spirit, groan inwardly while we wait for adoption, the redemption of our bodies. (Rom. 8:22-23)

In the same passage, Paul goes on to talk about the Spirit's interceding on our behalf "with sighs too deep for words" (v. 26). If one recognizes the work of the Spirit in the world, then one is motivated to join that great festive parade toward the wholeness and well-being of the whole of creation. Such a grand vision of the procession of the Spirit can motivate us to engage in solidarity and mutuality with others and thus fulfill our mission. It is a motivation that is not always certain about the details of the future; yet it is a motivation that knows the power of the Spirit which "blows where it chooses, and you hear the sound of it, but you do not know where it comes from or where it goes. So it is with everyone born of the Spirit" (John 3:8).

The word for Spirit in both Greek and Hebrew means "breath" or "wind." It is not a wind that blows one away; it is a wind that draws one toward itself. It is "lure" or "persuasive influence" that is operative in the work of the Spirit. The Holy Spirit, as it were, stands at the eschaton and draws the whole universe toward God and God's own Reign. Perhaps that is what Jesus meant when he said: "And I, when I am lifted up from the earth, will draw all people to myself" (John 12:32). This text does not merely refer to the event of the cross in which Jesus is lifted up like the brazen serpent in the wilderness; it refers much more strongly in the Johannine tradition to the work of the Holy Spirit in the world after the resurrection of Jesus from the dead.

As we can see, there is enough motivation—doxological, christological, soteriological, ecclesiological, and eschatological—available to us to engage in the kind of mission that we have outlined so far. How does one make such motivations become a reality in our congregations and parishes? Are we simply dealing with ideas that cannot be turned into concrete acts and programs? Are there practical ways in which one may engage in such motivation? The answer to these questions depends heavily on contextual issues. Questions such as which congregations, in which social locations, and in what kind of ministerial settings are some that need to be addressed. Each parish, church, and congregation is unique and peculiar in its life and practice. Therefore it is quite difficult, even impossible, to offer suggestions regarding practical ways to motivate people for a dialogical mission. We can only offer at this point some broad suggestions. Let me mention four such suggestions.

1. The theology of mission that we have outlined and the motivation for such mission requires a sustained theological education of the laity in the church. I do not mean those programs offered by the theological schools and seminaries under aegis of "lay theological education." What I mean is that each church should organize its educational program— Sunday classes, adult Bible study groups, children's education programs, preaching ministry—in such a way that it becomes a source for the education of Christians to venture into newer forms of missionary obedience. Such an educational process involves a rereading of our history and a reinterpretation of the Scriptures, as we have done here. Opportunities for such rethinking have to be intentionally created in our churches.

2. One of the ways in which the majority of Christians move into dialogical understanding of the mission of the church is through a flesh-and-blood encounter with people of other religions, such as Muslims, Jews, Hindus, and others. When people are exposed to others and enabled to enter into a face-to-face encounter with the religiosity and spirituality of the other, they are compelled to take that witness seriously and explore ways of offering one's own witness without negating the experience of the other. The wider circle of discussion that we have referred to will remain an empty idea until one actually participates in such a wider circle of conversation. It is one thing to talk about the religiously pluralistic world; it is an entirely different and often life-transforming matter when one meets a person of another faith who lives in cheerful obedience to God. Churches and congregations need

to intentionally create opportunities for such lively encounters with people of other religious persuasions.

3. More and more churches today are offering opportunities for their members to travel beyond the geographical confines of their church to churches in other regions, nations, and cultures. Thanks to the incredible advancement in the fields of transportation and communication, we can travel to other parts of the world in quicker and easier ways than our ancestors. Very often, such visits to places where Christians live and practice their Christian faith in different cultural and religious settings provide a keen motivation to engage in a mission of mutuality. One comes to understand and experience afresh the meaning of the confession "I believe in one, holy, *catholic* church." It offers a new way of perceiving the missionary task, very different from the simplistic vision of "sending" and "receiving." Mission becomes, in fact, mutual.

4. One of the structural changes that beg our attention regards the way in which the Board (Committee) of Mission and the Board (Committee) of Evangelism are kept separate in most churches. Such a structural arrangement has perpetuated the unhealthy division between mission and evangelism. It is has also perpetuated the view of mission as overseas mission and evangelism as membership drive. Churches need to seriously consider structurally incorporating these two so that one is enabled to view mission and evangelism as a whole.

The four suggestions put forward above are sketchy and do not exhaust the myriad of creative ways in which ministers and people can work together for a wider understanding of mission and thus motivate one another for actively involving in mission.

A final word. The theological exercise that we have been engaged in has argued for envisioning the mission of the church as a participation in a common task. It is a common task in that all humans are invited to own it for themselves and engage in it in collaborative and dialogical ways. The Christian faith offers a peculiar and unique perspective on what this common task is all about. So do other religious traditions and secular ideologies. Therefore, we come to this, "the common task," knowing that while we bring our own unique gifts, we are both aware and celebrative of our participating in a "common" task. It is a common task because it is God's task—a task that God has lovingly shared with all humans and the whole of creation.

Notes

Preface

1. Sheila G. Davaney, ed. (Philadelphia: Trinity Press International, 1991).

Introduction

1. I am depending on *World Missionary Conference, 1910, The History and Records of the Conference Together with Addresses Delivered at the Evening Meetings* (New York: Fleming H. Revell Co.), for the statistical information used in this section.

2. See Pauline Webb, "Women in Church and Society," *Dictionary of the Ecumenical Movement,* ed. Nicholas Lossky et al. (Grand Rapids, Mich.: Eerdmans, 1991), which discusses the role of women in the missionary movement. There is also a full issue of *International Review of Mission* dedicated to the issue of women in mission. See vol. LXXXI, No. 322, April 1992.

3. *San Antonio Report,* Frederick R. Wilson, ed. (Geneva: WCC, 1990), pp. 6-7.

4. The Inter-Church Center at 475 Riverside Drive, New York, has been housing the mission societies of the various Protestant denominations of this country for decades. Though some of these offices have shifted to other places in recent times, the Inter-Church Center, even today, symbolizes the hub of missionary thinking and activity.

5. Rebecca S. Chopp, *Saving Work: Feminist Practices of Theological Education* (Louisville: Westminster John Knox Press, 1995), p. ix.

6. Theologians like Aloysius Pieris of Sri Lanka, Raymond Panikkar of India, and others have made important contributions to this discussion. See writings by Pieris including *An Asian Theology of Liberation* (New York: Orbis Books, 1990), and books by Panikkar including *The Unknown Christ of Hinduism: Toward an Ecumenical Christophany* (New York: Orbis Books, 1981).

7. David Bosch, *Transforming Mission: Paradigm Shifts in Theology of Mission* (New York: Orbis Books, 1991), p. 336.

8. Timothy Yates, *Christian Mission in the Twentieth Century* (Cambridge: Cambridge University Press, 1994), p. 200.

9. Bosch, *Transforming Mission,* p. 334.

10. Ibid., p. 338.

11. World Missionary Conference, 1910, *History and Records,* p. 108.

12. Ibid., p. 348.

13. Karl Barth, *The Epistle to the Romans* (London: Oxford University Press, 1968), p. 28.

14. James A. Scherer, *Gospel, Church, and Kingdom: Comparative Studies in World Mission Theology* (Minneapolis: Augsburg Publishing House, 1987), p. 22.

15. They believed that their colonial and commercial expansion went hand in hand with propagating the gospel among the natives in the colonies. As David Bosch puts it, "Colonialism and mission, as a matter of course, were interdependent; the right to have colonies carried with it the duty to Christianize the colonized" (David Bosch, *Transforming Mission,* p. 227).

16. Ibid., p. 303.

17. Ibid., p. 305.

18. Stephen Neill, *A History of Christian Missions,* rev. ed. (New York: Penguin Books, 1986), p. 414.

19. Ibid., p. 418.

20. Gary Laderman, ed. *Religions of Atlanta: Religious Diversity in the Centennial Olympic City* (Atlanta: Scholars Press, 1996).

21. Ibid., p. 3.

22. Andrew Wingate, *Encounter in the Spirit: Muslim-Christian Meetings in Birmingham* (Geneva: WCC, 1988), p. 4.

23. As quoted in James A. Joseph, "Pluralism and Civil Society: The Changing Civil Society," ed. W. Lawson Taitte, *Individualism and Social Responsibility* (Dallas: University of Texas, 1994), pp. 171-83.

24. James Scherer, *Gospel, Church, and Kingdom,* p. 33.

25. Ibid.

26. David Lyon, *Postmodernity* (Minneapolis: University of Minnesota Press, 1994), p. 12.

27. Ibid.

28. Peter C. Hodgson, *Winds of the Spirit: A Constructive Christian Theology* (Louisville: Westminster John Knox Press, 1994), p. 56.

29. Hodgson discusses all the seven crises in pp. 56-61.

30. Ibid., p. 60.

31. Valson Thambu, *Rediscovering Mission: Toward a Non-Western Missiological Paradigm* (New Delhi: TRACI, 1995).

32. Meenakshi is the name of the presiding goddess in the largest Hindu temple in Madurai, and the Hindu Mission hospital is, in a sense, the Hindu counterpart of the Christian Mission hospital, which was started by the Christian missionaries several decades ago.

33. New York: Orbis Books, 1990. See pp. 2-18.

34. For example, see C. S. Song, *Third-Eye Theology: Theology in Formation in Asian Settings* (New York: Orbis Books, 1979), and Kosuke Koyama, *Mount Fuji and Mount Sinai—A Pilgrimage in Theology* (London: SCM Press, 1984).

35. For example, see Rebecca Chopp, *Saving Work*, p. 21.

36. Hugald Grafe, *History of Christianity in India: Volume IV, Part 2, Tamilnadu in the Nineteenth and Twentieth Centuries* (Bangalore, India: Church History Association of India, 1990), p. 27.

37. Peter Hodgson, *Winds of the Spirit*, p. 101.

38. Gordon D. Kaufman, *In Face of Mystery: A Constructive Theology* (Cambridge, Mass.: Harvard University Press, 1993), p. 66.

1. A New Starting Point

1. Hans-Georg Gadamer, *Truth and Method* (New York: Crossroad, 1982), p. 330.

2. Ibid., p. 337.

3. Ibid., p. 341.

4. Ibid., p. 345.

5. Gordon D. Kaufman, *In Face of Mystery* (Cambridge, Mass.: Harvard University Press, 1993), p. 19.

6. Paul Tillich, *Systematic Theology*, vol. 1 (Chicago: University of Chicago Press, 1951), p. 34.

7. John Macquarrie, *Principles of Christian Theology* (London: SCM Press, 1966), p. 4.

8. "The Church in the World: Rethinking the Great Commission," *Theology Today*, XLVII, no. 4 (January 1991), p. 410.

9. "Reading Luke from the Perspective of Liberation Theology," *Text and Interpretation: New Approaches in the Criticism of the New Testament*, ed. P. J. Hartin and J. H. Petzer (Leiden: E. J. Brill, 1991), p. 281.

10. For example see John R. W. Stott, *Christian Mission in the Modern World: What the Church Should Be Doing Now!* (Downers Grove, Ill.: Inter-Varsity Press, 1975), p. 22, and Robert E. Coleman, *The Great Commission Lifestyle: Conforming Your Life to Kingdom Priorities* (Grand Rapids, Mich.: Fleming H. Revell, 1992).

11. For example, see: "Your Kingdom Come: Melbourne, 1980 (World Conference on Mission and Evangelism)" *New Directions in Mission and Evangelization: Basic Documents 1974–1991*, ed. James A. Scherer and Stephen B. Bevans (New York: Orbis Books, 1992), pp. 27–35.

12. *The Ecumenical Movement: An Anthology of Key Texts and Voices*, ed. Michael Kinnamon and Brian E. Cope (Geneva: WCC Publications, 1997), p. 465.

13. Rebecca Chopp, *Saving Work: Feminist Practices of Theological Education* (Louisville: Westminster John Knox Press, 1995), p. 46.

14. Ibid.

15. David Bosch, *Transforming Mission: Paradigm Shifts in Theology of Mission* (New York: Orbis Books, 1991), p. 389.

16. Ibid., p. 391.

17. Ibid.

18. One can notice this clearly in the Manifesto of the Communist Party. See *Marx & Engels: Basic Writings on Politics and Philosophy*, ed. Lewis S. Feuer (New York: Doubleday, 1959), pp. 1-41.

19. Gordon D. Kaufman, *God, Mystery, Diversity: Christian Theology in a Pluralistic World* (Minneapolis: Fortress Press, 1996), p. 56.

20. Alec Irwin, "Face of Mystery, Mystery of a Face: An Anthropological Trajectory in Wittgenstein, Cavell, and Kaufman Biohistorical Theology," *Harvard Theological Review*, 88, no. 3 (1995), p. 391.

21. I am heavily dependent here on Kaufman's latest writing, *In Face of Mystery: A Constructive Theology*. Since he has worked these out in a fuller fashion, I will not engage in a detailed discussion, but I will mention the three affirmations and expound them briefly.

22. Manfred Frank, "Is Subjectivity a Non-Thing, an Absurdity [Unding]? On Some Difficulties in Naturalistic Reductions of Self-Consciousness," in *The Modern Subject: Conceptions of the Self in Classical German Philosophy*, ed. Karl Ameriks and Dieter Sturma (New York: SUNY Press, 1995), p. 185.

23. Kaufman, *In Face of Mystery*, p. 106.

2. *Missio Humanitatis*

1. David Bosch, *Transforming Mission: Paradigm Shifts in Theology of Mission* (New York: Orbis, 1991), p. 1.

2. H. Richard Niebuhr, *The Responsible Self: An Essay in Christian Moral Philosophy* (New York: Harper & Row, 1963).

3. Gordon D. Kaufman, *In Face of Mystery: A Constructive Theology* (Cambridge, Mass.: Harvard University Press, 1993), p. 141.

4. The discussion of Niebuhr's ideas on "responsibility" is based solely on the chapter "The Meaning of Responsibility" in *The Responsible Self*, p. 47.

5. Niebuhr, *The Responsible Self*, p. 61.

6. Ibid., pp. 63-64.

7. Ibid., p. 65.

8. William Schweiker, *Responsibility and Christian Ethics* (Cambridge: Cambridge University Press, 1995), chapter 4.

9. Ibid., p. 86.

10. Ibid., p. 95.

11. Niebuhr, *The Responsible Self*, pp. 69-89.

12. Ibid., p. 78.

13. Sarvepalli Radhakrishnan and Charles A. Moore, ed. *A Sourcebook in Indian Philosophy* (Princeton: Princeton University Press, 1957), p. 190.

14. Ruy O. Costa, "Introduction," *Struggles for Solidarity: Liberation Theologies in Tension*, Lorine M. Getz and Ruy O. Costa, ed. (Minneapolis: Augsburg Fortress Press, 1991), p. 20.

15. As quoted by Kathleen Talvacchia, "Learning to Stand with Others Through Compassionate Solidarity," *Union Seminary Quarterly Review* 47, nos. 3-4 (1993), p. 179.

16. You can find this reference in Ada Maria Isasi-Diaz, "Solidarity: Love of Neighbor in the 1980s," *Lift Every Voice: Constructing Christian Theology from the Underside*, ed. Susan B. Thistlethwaite and Mary P. Engel (San Francisco: Harper Collins, 1990), pp. 31-40.

17. Ibid., pp. 32-33.

18. Darlene Ehinger, "Toward an Ethic of Mutuality: An Integrated Concept of Justice," *Sewanee Theological Review*, 36, no. 3 (Pentecost 1993), p. 410.

19. James W. Fowler, *Stages of Faith: The Psychology of Human*

Development and the Quest for Meaning (New York: Harper & Row, 1981), p. 121 (italics mine).

20. Leonard Swidler, "Mutuality: The Matrix for Mature Living, Some Philosophical and Christian Theological Reflections," *Religion & Intellectual Life*, III, no. 1 (Fall 1985), pp. 105-119.

3. Missio Ecclesiae

1. Gordon Kaufman, *In Face of Mystery: A Constructive Theology* (Cambridge, Mass.: Harvard University Press, 1993), p. 83.

2. David C. Scott, ed. *Keshub Chunder Sen* (Madras, India: Christian Literature Society, 1979), p. 228.

3. Ibid.

4. Karl Barth, *Church Dogmatics, Vol. 1, Pt. 1: Doctrine of the Word of God, Prolegomena to Church Dogmatics* (Edinburgh: T & T Clark, 1975), pp. 22-24.

5. Kosuke Koyama, *Three Mile an Hour God: Biblical Reflections* (New York: Orbis Books, 1979), pp. 51-55.

6. Elizabeth Moltman-Wendel, "Is There a Feminist Theology of the Cross?" *The Scandal of a Crucified World: Perspectives on the Cross and Suffering,* ed. Jacob Tesfai (New York, Orbis Books, 1994), pp. 87-98.

7. Ibid., p. 87.

8. Roberta C. Bondi, *Memories of God: Theological Reflection on a Life* (Nashville: Abingdon Press, 1995), pp. 111-44.

9. David C. Scott, ed. *Keshub Chunder Sen* (Madras, India: Christian Literature Society, 1979), p. 48.

10. R. H. S. Boyd, *An Introduction to Indian Christian Theology* (New Delhi: ISPCK, 1989), p. 182.

11. M. M. Thomas, *Faith and Ideology in the Struggle for Justice*, Bishop Joshi Memorial Lectures 1984 (Bombay: BUILD, 1984), p. 4.

12. D. J. Smit, "Morality and Individual Responsibility," *Journal of Theology for Southern Africa*, no. 89 (December 1994), p. 21.

13. Moltman-Wendel, "Is There a Feminist Theology of the Cross?" p. 95.

14. Elizabeth A. Johnson, *She Who Is: The Mystery of God in Feminist Theological Discourse* (New York: Crossroad, 1992), p. 266.

15. Ibid., p. 267.

16. Since the publication of the book *The Myth of God Incarnate* by

John Hick in 1977, there has been a significant amount of discussion on the nature and meaning of incarnation. I do not go into that discussion here.

17. Kathleen Talvacchia, "Learning to Stand with Others Through Compassionate Solidarity," *Union Seminary Quarterly Review* 47, no. 3-4 (1993), p. 192.

18. As quoted by Elizabeth Johnson, *She Who Is*, p. 267.

19. George E. Tinker, "Blessed Are the Poor: A Theology of Solidarity with the Poor in the Two-Thirds World," *Church and Society* 84, (March-April 1994), p. 49.

20. Ibid., p. 49.

21. Talvacchia, "Learning to Stand with Others Through Compassionate Solidarity," p. 184.

4. Issues in Mission

1. William J. Richardson, *Social Action Vs. Evangelism: An Essay on the Contemporary Crisis* (South Pasadena: William Carey Library, 1977), p. 26.

2. John Power, *Mission Theology Today* (New York: Orbis Books, 1971), p. 159.

3. H. Eddie Fox and George Morris, *Faith-Sharing: Dynamic Christian Witnessing by Invitation* (Nashville: Discipleship Resources, 1986), p. 44.

4. David Bosch, *Transforming Mission: Paradigm Shifts in Theology of Mission* (New York: Orbis Books, 1991), pp. 411-20.

5. Kenneth Cracknell, *Protestant Evangelism or Catholic Evangelization?* (England: The Methodist Sacramental Fellowship, 1992), p. 3.

6. Mark 1:15. See also Acts 15:7; Rom.1:16; Matt.4:23; and so on.

7. David Bosch, *Transforming Mission*, p. 411.

8. Ibid., p. 415.

9. David Bosch, "The Vulnerability of Mission," *New Directions in Mission & Evangelism, No. 2: Theological Foundations*, ed. James Scherer and Stephen Bevans (New York: Orbis Books, 1994), p. 83.

10. Donald A. McGavran, *Understanding Church Growth* (Grand Rapids, Mich.: Eerdmans, 1970), p. 49.

11. Ibid., p. 63.

12. Diogenes Allen, *Three Outsiders* (Cambridge, Mass.: Cowley Publications, 1983), p. 97.

13. Kenneth Cracknell, *Protestant Evangelism or Catholic Evangelization?* p. 19.

14. As quoted by M. M. Thomas, *The Acknowledged Christ of the Indian Renaissance,* 2nd ed. (Madras: Christian Literature Society, 1976), p. 209.

15. Stanley Jones, *Conversion* (Nashville: Abingdon Press, 1959).

16. Ibid., p. 46.

17. M. M. Thomas, *Faith and Ideology in the Struggle for Justice* (Bombay, BUILD, 1984), p. 4.

18. David Bosch, *Transforming Mission,* p. xv.

19. Ibid.

20. E. Stanley Jones, *Conversion,* p. 52.

21. Romans 12:2 (italics mine).

22. "Communities of Collaboration: Shared Commitments/Common Tasks," *Theology at the End of Modernity,* ed. Sheila G. Davaney (Philadelphia: Trinity International, 1991), p. 201.

23. Wesley Granberg-Michaelson, *Redeeming the Creation: The Rio Earth Summit: Challenges to the Churches* (Geneva, WCC, 1992), p. vi.

24. Refer to my unpublished paper, "Evangelism as Emmanuelization of Creation" (presented at the Mission Evangelism Consultation for Professors of Mission, Evangelism, and Related Theological Fields, sponsored by The General Board of Global Ministries, Leesburg, Fla., January 1997).

25. "Orthodox Theology and the Problems of the Environment," *The Greek Orthodox Theological Review,* 38, nos. 1-4 (1993), p. 175.

26. Wesley Ariarajah, *The Bible and People of Other Faiths* (Geneva: World Council of Churches, 1985), p. 44.

27. World Council of Churches, *Guidelines on Dialogue with People of Living Faiths and Ideologies* (Geneva: WCC, 1979).

28. M. Thomas Thangaraj, *The Crucified Guru: An Experiment in Cross-Cultural Christology* (Nashville: Abingdon Press, 1994).

29. Francis X. Clooney, *Seeing Through Texts: Doing Theology Among the Srivaishnavas of South India* (New York: SUNY Press, 1996).

30. Jose Kuttianimattathil, *Practice and Theology of Interreligious Dialogue: A Critical Study of the Indian Christian Attempts Since Vatican II* (Bangalore, India: Kristu Jyoti Publications, 1995), p. 635.

31. "The Lausanne Covenant," *New Directions in Mission and Evangelization: Basic Documents 1972–1991,* ed. James Scherer and Stephen Bevans (New York: Orbis Books, 1992), p. 255.

32. James A. Scherer and Stephen B. Bevans, ed., *New Directions in Mission and Evangelism: Basic Documents 1972–1991* (New York: Orbis Books, 1992), p. 187.

33. Wesley Ariarajah, *The Bible and People of Other Faiths*, p. 39.

5. Rereading Our History

1. Pelican Books, 1986.

2. Timothy Yates, *Christian Mission in the Twentieth Century* (Cambridge: Cambridge University Press, 1994).

3. David Bosch, *Transforming Mission: Paradigm Shifts in Theology of Mission* (New York: Orbis Books, 1991), p. 207.

4. "Go Forth in Peace: Orthodox Perspectives on Mission, 1986," *New Directions in Mission and Evangelization: Basic Documents 1972–1991*, ed. Scherer and Bevans (New York: Orbis Books, 1992), p. 213.

5. Yates, *Christian Mission in the Twentieth Century*, pp. 138-55.

6. See Vincent Cronin, *A Pearl to India: The Life of Robert De Nobili* (New York: Dutton, 1959).

7. See Vincent Donovan, *Rediscovering Christianity* (London: SCM Press, 1978).

8. "Early Christian Persecutions," *The Oxford Dictionary of the Christian Church*, ed. F. L. Cross (London: Oxford University Press, 1958), p. 1047.

9. One such village is Mudalur in Tirunelveli District of Tamilnadu, India, where the missionaries settled the new converts in a new plot of land and called that Mudalur ("first town"). See Hugald Grafe, *History of Christianity in India, Volume V, Part 2: Tamilnadu in the Nineteenth and Twentieth Centuries* (Bangalore, India: Church History Association of India, 1990), p. 27.

10. See Stephen Neill, *A History of Christian Missions*, rev. ed. (New York: Penguin Books, 1986).

11. Robin Boyd, *An Introduction to Christian Theology* (New Delhi: ISPCK, 1989), p. 15.

12. David Bosch, *Transforming Mission*, p. 310.

13. See Neill, *A History of Christian Missions*, p. 54.

14. Ibid., p. 97.

15. Ibid., p. 68.

16. Ibid., p. 59.

17. Ibid., p. 72.

18. A facsimile of this booklet was later published by the Baptist Missionary Society (London, 1942).

19. As quoted by Robin Boyd, *An Introduction to Indian Christian Theology* (Madras: CLS, 1975), p. 15.

20. Kenneth Cracknell, *Justice, Courtesy and Love: Theologians and Missionaries Encountering World Religions, 1846–1914* (London: Epworth Press, 1995).

21. Hugald Grafe, *History of Christianity in India: Volume IV, Part 2, Tamilnadu in the Nineteenth and Twentieth Centuries* (Bangalore, India: Church History Association of India, 1990), p. 60.

22. Madras: Christian Literature Society for India, 1902.

23. Ibid., p. 69.

24. David Bosch, *Transforming Mission*, p. 286.

25. Translated by Myra Bergman Ramos (New York: Seabury Press, 1974).

26. *A History of Christian Missions*, p. 401.

6. Reinterpreting the Bible

1. New York: Orbis Books, 1983.

2. Robin Boyd, *An Introduction to Indian Christian Theology* (New Delhi: ISPCK, 1989), p. 34.

3. Genesis 3:16-19.

4. See Micah 6:6, Isaiah 1:12, and Jeremiah 7:1 and 29:7.

5. Senior and Stuhlmueller, *The Biblical Foundations for Mission*, p. 142.

6. Mortimer Arias has ably argued for the centrality of the idea of the Reign of God for the understanding and practice of evangelism in his book, titled *Announcing the Reign of God: Evangelization and the Subversive Memory of Jesus* (Philadelphia: Augsburg Fortress Press, 1984).

7. Matthew 22:1-10 and Luke 14:16-24.

8. Matthew 28:16.

9. David Bosch, *Transforming Mission: Paradigm Shifts in Theology of Mission* (New York: Orbis Books, 1991), p. 50.

10. Robin Boyd, *An Introduction to Christian Theology*, p. 159.

11. See Revelation 21:22.

12. The two books where this is specifically addressed are: Wesley Ariarajah, *The Bible and the People of Other Faiths* (Geneva: WCC, 1985),

and Kenneth Cracknell, *Towards a New Relationship: Christians and People of Other Faith* (London: Epworth Press, 1986).

13. See John 12:27 and 13:21.

14. Jay B. McDaniel, *With Roots and Wings: Christianity in an Age of Ecology and Dialogue* (New York: Orbis Books, 1995).

7. Motivating for Mission

1. Alan Walker, *The New Evangelism* (Nashville: Abingdon Press, 1975), p. 9.

2. Mortimer Arias, "The Church in the World: Rethinking the Great Commission," *Theology Today*, XLVII, no. 4 (January 1991), p. 415.

3. Michael Green, *Evangelism in the Early Church* (Grand Rapids, Mich.: Eerdmans, reprint, 1982), p. 236.

4. *Faith-Sharing: Dynamic Christian Witnessing by Invitation* (Nashville: Discipleship Resources, 1986), p. 12.

5. *Model of the Church* (New York: Image Books, extended edition, 1987).

6. For example, see Matthew 25.

7. See Luke 15.